PATHWAYS TO MATURITY: INSIGHTS FROM A THIRTY-YEAR STUDY OF DEPRIVED CHILDREN

In the world of child development, the conventional wisdom has been that children severely deprived in their earliest years do not regain the losses suffered, no matter what their later upbringing. *Pathways to Maturity* presents a model for psychological rehabilitation of deprived institutionalized children which not only explodes the myth but shows how significant rehabilitation can be accomplished and offers intriguing insights into the complexities of human development.

The study describes, in the first stage, the serious developmental and mental health deficits of a group of 85 infants being reared in an institution in Toronto in 1956. The children had no close relationships, no toys or possessions, and no interaction with the other children, and spent most of their waking hours in bed, seldom outside their nursery and never outdoors. Speech was non-existent and vocalization infrequent. They had limited motor skills, grossly retarded intellectual development, and an inability to relate to adults or peers, which precluded successful placement in foster or adoptive homes.

In the second stage, involving 28 of these children, aged three months to three years, rehabilitative treatment was undertaken to prepare the children for placement. The authors outline intervention strategies and therapeutic techniques used and discuss the ongoing adaptation of the children to home, school, and community, under the guidance of a case worker, until they reached the ages of 15 to 18 years.

In the third stage of the study, 22 of the original 28 were located and interviewed regarding their lifestyles, coping strategies, and mental health as young adults, then aged 28 through 31 years. While the individuals involved showed many different ways of maturing, their histories consistently demonstrated the value of professional support in helping deprived children to overcome adversity. In effect, *Pathways to Maturity* is a tribute to the resilience of the human spirit.

BETTY M. FLINT is Professor Emerita in the Institute of Child Study at the Faculty of Education, University of Toronto. She is author of several books, including *New Hope for Deprived Children* and *The Flint Infant Security Scale*.
JEAN G. PARTRIDGE, C. Psych., is a Research Associate at the Institute of Child Study at the Faculty of Education, University of Toronto.
ELIZABETH G. STARK, now retired, was Coordinator of Psychological Services, Catholic Children's Aid, Toronto.

BETTY M. FLINT
JEAN G. PARTRIDGE
ELIZABETH G. STARK

Pathways to Maturity: Insights from a Thirty-Year Study of Deprived Children

UNIVERSITY OF TORONTO PRESS
Toronto Buffalo London

© University of Toronto Press Incorporated 1996
Toronto Buffalo London
Printed in Canada

ISBN 0-8020-0785-6 (cloth)
ISBN 0-8020-7148-1 (paper)

Printed on acid-free paper

Canadian Cataloguing in Publication Data

Flint, Betty, M., 1920–
  Pathways to maturity : insights from a thirty year study
  of deprived children

  Includes bibliographical references and index.
  ISBN 0-8020-0785-6 (bound) ISBN 0-8020-7148-1 (pbk.)

  1. Children – Institutional care – Canada – Longitudinal
  studies.   2. Children, Adopted – Canada – Longitudinal
  studies.   3. Adoptees – Canada – Longitudinal studies.
  I. Partridge, Jean, G.   II. Stark, Elizabeth G.
  III. Title

  HV887.C3F58 1996   362.7'3   C95-933374-6

University of Toronto Press acknowledges the financial assistance to its
publishing program of the Canada Council and the Ontario Arts Council.

This book has been published with the help of a grant from the Humanities
and Social Sciences Federation of Canada, using funds provided by the Social
Sciences and Humanities Research Council of Canada.

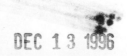

Contents

vi   Pathways to Maturity

Foreword

This book reports a rare long-term charting of individual life paths. It is a good book about children and how important commitment is to their lives. It is a story of childhood adversity that has a largely happy outcome. The study describes a rescue operation with 85 children that ranged from three months to three and one-half years of age. These children were found in the circumstance of being in an institution that as a matter of policy provided for only their most basic needs and, by that, deprived them of most normal social contacts and emotional experiences. The life stories assembled and described here by Professor Flint and her colleagues present a cohort of children that were systematically followed from the discovery of their plight in 1956, to their subsequent foster placement, through adoption, adolescence, and into their early adult life 30 years later.

Time, place, and people play major roles in the course that a human life takes. Few researchers have had the courage and tenacity to sample and follow some of the diverse pathways that are possible. Even fewer researchers assume the added responsibility of becoming significant interveners and engineers in the course of other people's lives. To undertake such sustained study, systematize what was learned, and write this book took a remarkable team.

Although a social service agency oversaw the children's care plan, it was the Flint team that carried out assessments, planned treatment, and implemented the intervention. Mary Kilgour was the first to encounter the children. In 1955 Mary was supplementing her obstetrical nursing training with courses in social work and child study offered by the University of Toronto. As part of her course work she came into contact with the children and their deprived condition. Because of her observations and reports she was appointed director of the home until its closing in 1959. At that time, Professor Flint began to obtain what would be 20 years of funding to study the children's lives. After the home closed Mary became the project's guidance worker for the duration of the study. She supervised the placements, adoptions, and support of the children and their new families. Many of the relationships Mary established were so positive that they continue today. In 1988 Mary came out of retirement to help in the location and follow-up of the children. She and Jean Partridge interviewed the study participants, who were then between 28 and 31 years of age.

Jean Partridge had been associated with the University of Toronto as a research associate and lecturer since 1943. In 1987 she joined the Flint team to help locate study participants, develop the interview schedule, and carry out some of the interviews. During her long involvement with the Institute she became familiar with the ideas and approach to conceptualizing research known as security theory. This approach was elaborated through the project and became the major tool for making sense of the data that emerged from the follow-up interviews.

Betty Stark studied at the Institute of Child Study after raising six children. Through her work in parent education she became familiar with security theory and had worked with Jean Partridge and Betty Flint in the development of the Flint Infant Security Scale. This expertise was added to the Flint follow-up team in 1987.

The team leader, Professor Betty Flint, came to the Institute with a background in history. Flint's involvement in a war-time nursery led her to see the link between history and child development. She obtained a Diploma in Child Study in 1946 and a Master's Degree in psychology in 1948. The year after graduation she went to work in children's services. After making important contributions for over a decade to both that area and the field of early childhood education, she began in 1956 the intervention and research that have been the subject of this and three previous books (Flint, 1959; 1963; 1978). Through her writing, lectures, and consultations, Professor Flint's work provides a solid basis for optimism about ways that human interventions can support the remarkable adaptability and strength of the human spirit.

The largely positive developmental trajectories of the children portrayed in this book are further evidence of what H.S. Sullivan (1953) described as the 'tendency toward health.' This view assumes that there is a basic tendency in all persons toward emotional and interpersonal health. Interventions are seen not as cures but, rather, as efforts to remove obstacles that hinder the natural direction of adaptation and development. Sullivan's favourite metaphor to illustrate this point was that the problem in a garden is not the flowers but the weeds. Eliminate the weeds and the flowers will grow.

This research joins a number of long-term outcome studies that dramatically portray the astonishing adaptive capacities of children. Anna Freud (1961) reported how children endured the relentless bombing runs over England. Eisen (1988) recorded how young children in Nazi concentration camps used play activities to help withstand the horror of daily deprivation and death. Lappin (1963) chronicled how the Canadian Jewish Congress War Orphans Rescue Movement came to the aid of young war victims by resettling them in Canada. In spite of predictions that the horror of their experiences would debilitate them for life, these survivors coped with their past and adapted admirably to life in Canada.

More directly, there has been a great deal of recent interest in examining foster care and adoption outcomes. Most of the outcomes report that children once in foster care appear to remain in care. This is especially true for children that are not returned to the biological parents within two or three years. Because children in care have been abused or neglected and because care experiences are often aversive, there is a widespread perception that children who experience foster care placement are at great risk for poor mental health outcomes. Existing follow-up studies, although unable to sort out the consequences of pre- and post-placement experiences, do not support this perception. Studies consistently report no pronounced negative effects of short-term foster care on later life adaptation (Fanshel & Shinn, 1978; Triselotis, 1980; Festinger, 1983; Leavey, 1987; Fanshel, 1989). Maluccio and Fein (1985) conclude in their review that current research does 'not support the prevailing wisdom regarding the widespread negative impact of growing up in foster care.' More recently these authors, Fein and Maluccio (1991), assert that 'follow up studies suggest that the initial negative effects of separation and placement in foster care can be counteracted or reduced through the influence of stable foster home placements and strong services to the children and their foster and biological parents.'

Foster care is not the same as adoption. The children described by Flint in this outcome study experienced both foster and adoptive care. Adoptive care provided them with parents and permanent homes.

Foster care is usually provided for children who cannot grow up with their biological parents because of neglect, abandonment, or abuse. Moreover, fostering, in contrast to adoption, is most often thought of as temporary. Although adopted children are over-represented in both child and adult clinical populations (Bohman & von Knotting, 1979; Brinich & Brinich, 1982; Brodzinsky, 1987), adoption still appears to be a better situation for children than long-term foster care (Trisleiotis & Hill, 1990). Bohman and Sigvardsson (1990) conclude on the basis of their own longitudinal research that the long-term prognosis for adopted children is no worse than for other children if parents are prepared for the task of rearing an adopted child. The life stories told in the following chapters attest to the Flint team's ability to provide and sustain such preparation.

Although controversy surrounds explanations as to what fortifies the resilient and invulnerable child, this book provides evidence that systems of influence, both inside, outside, and among people operate to shape their actions, activities, challenges, opportunities, and choices. It is these systems that constitute the life stories and their lessons so effectively told herein.

Richard Volpe, Ph.D.
   Director, The Dr R.G.N. Laidlaw Centre
Institute of Child Study
University of Toronto

References

Bohman, M., & Sigvardsson, S. (1978). An 18 year prospective, longitudinal study of adopted boys. In E. Anthony, C. Koupernik, & C. Chiland (Eds.), *The child in his family: Vulnerable children*. Vol. 4. New York: Wiley.

Bohman, M., & Sigvardsson, S. (1990). Outcome in adoption: Lessons from longitudinal studies. In D. Brodzinsky and M. Hall (Eds.), *The psychology of adoption*. Oxford: Oxford University Press.

Brinich, P., & Brinich, E. (1982). Adoption and adaptation. *Journal of Nervous and Mental Disorder*, *170*, 489–93.

Brodzinsky, D. (1987). Adjustment to adoption: A psychosocial perspective. *Clinical Psychology Review*, 7, 25–47.

Eisen, G. (1988). *Children and play in the holocaust*. Amherst: The University of Massachusetts.

Fanshel, D., & Shinn, E. (1978). *Children in foster care – A longitudinal investigation.* New York: Columbia University Press.

Fanshel, D. (1989). Foster children in life course perspective. *Child Welfare,* 68(5), 467–78.

Festinger, T. (1983). No one ever asked us ... A postscript to foster care. *American Journal of Orthopsychiatry, 50,* 256–63.

Fein, E., & Maluccio, A. (1991). Foster family care: Solution or problem. In R. Brown & W. Brown (Eds.), *Why some children succeed despite all odds.* New York: Praeger.

Flint, B. (1959). *The security of infants.* Toronto: University of Toronto Press.

Flint, B. (1966). *The child and the institution.* Toronto: University of Toronto Press.

Flint, B. (1978). *New hope for deprived children.* Toronto: University of Toronto Press.

Goldstein, J., Freud, A., & Solnit, A. (1973). *Beyond the best interests of the child.* New York: Free Press.

Lappin, B. (1963). *The redeemed children.* Toronto: University of Toronto Press.

Leavey, J.M. (1987). *Commission on foster care. A final report.* Boston: Boston Co. & Communities for People, Inc.

Maluccio, A. & Fein, E. (1985). Growing up in foster care. *Children and Youth Services Review, 7,* 123–34.

Sullivan, H.S. (1953). *The interpersonal theory of psychiatry.* New York: Norton.

Triseliotis, J. (1980). Growing up in foster care and after. In J. Triseliotis (Ed.), *New developments in foster care and adoption.* London: Routledge & Kegan Paul.

Triseliotis, J., & Hill, M. (1990). Contrasting adoption, foster care, and residential rearing. In D. Brodzinsky and M. Hall (Eds.), *The psychology of adoption.* Oxford: Oxford University Press.

Preface

This venture began as a pure research project, continued as a human rescue operation, and unfolded in its final stage as a revelation of human potential. It has enriched the knowledge of its investigators and the quality of life of its subjects. The insights shared have been the ultimate reward of this enterprise.

The story unfolds in three phases; the first describes the serious developmental and mental health deficits of a group of 85 infants being reared in an extremely depriving institution.

The second and longest phase involved the rehabilitation treatment that prepared the children for foster or adoptive homes and described the ongoing adaptation of 28 of them to home, school, and community until they were 15 through 18 years of age.

The third phase involved a search for our subjects when they were 28 through 31 years of age. Twenty were interviewed about their lifestyle, their coping strategies, and their mental health as young adults.

Since the inception of our project, scholarly investigations into issues of deprivation have shifted in focus from client vulnerability to client resilience, opposite ends of the spectrum of human adaptation. Both these qualities were observed in our subjects from the project's beginning in 1956 to its termination in 1988. Our close association with our subjects and their families has permitted us some insight into the factors that influence these qualities.

My long career as a teacher and researcher has allowed for reflection and re-evaluation regarding the implications of this study. This process has been documented in three previous books. Presented here are the results of 40 years' fascination with the unfolding development of a special group of children and the insights gained from their lives.

Acknowledgments

Many colleagues and Research Associates at the Institute of Child Study have contributed substantial skills and time to this study. The late Dr Mary Northway, Professor Dorothy Millichamp, Dr Bruce Quarrington, Mrs June Edmonds, Mrs Jean Partridge, Dr Ann Taylor, and Mrs Betty Stark have taken part at different times over the past 30 years. Most important has been the 30-year commitment of Miss Mary Kilgour, whose efforts were a powerful catalyst in the rehabilitation of these children and whose continuing interest in their welfare enabled us to locate many of them after a 15-year interval. The late W. Ward Markle, as Executive Director, ensured the cooperation and support of the Catholic Children's Aid Society through the early stages of this joint venture.

This study has been supported from 1956–74 and 1983–85 by the following agencies:

The Laidlaw Foundation
The Ontario Mental Health Foundation
The Atkinson Charitable Foundation
The Neathern Foundation
The Blatz Foundation
National Health and Welfare Canada
The B & B Foundation
The University of Toronto
The Social Science Research Council of Canada
The Publications Fund of the University of Toronto Press

Betty M. Flint
Professor Emerita
Institute of Child Study
Faculty of Education
University of Toronto
May 1995

Sequence of Events, 1956–93

Phase I

1956   A study of the mental health of 16 institutionalized infants in order to validate the Flint Infant Security Scale.

A dramatic decline in mental health was demonstrated; illness became increasingly severe the longer the infant remained in the institution. C.A. 3 mos – 24 mos.

1957–58   An assessment of the environmental deficiencies within the institution and the implications for the group of 85 children. C.A. 3 mos. – 3.5 years.

Reported in: Flint, B.M. (1959). *The security of infants.* Toronto: University of Toronto Press.

Phase II

1957–78   Modification of the environment, the creation of a therapeutic milieu, and the children's response.

Reported in: Flint, B.M. (1966). *The child and the institution: A study of deprivation and recovery.* Toronto: University of Toronto Press.

Placement of the children in homes and continuous guidance and evaluation of 28 selected subjects until they were 15–18 years.

Reported in: Flint, B.M. (1978). *New hope for deprived chil-dren.* Toronto: University of Toronto Press.

Phase III

1988–93   Evaluation of the subjects' adaptation as adults. Location of 20 of the original 28 selected subjects for interviews at ages 28–31 years. Longitudinal analysis of case histories from infancy through adulthood of 20 subjects.

Satellite Study of a Contrast Group

1989–92   Retrieval of microfiche longitudinal data on 14 subjects who shared the same institutional deprivation as the experimental subjects but who had grown to maturity within the traditional foster care system.

PATHWAYS TO MATURITY

1

Telling the Story

When this study was initiated in 1956,[1] the subjects were a group of 85 children ranging in age from three months to three and one-half years of age. They were residents in a long-standing institution in Toronto, Canada, that offered substitute care to children under the supervision of the Catholic Children's Aid Society (CCAS). At this time, welfare agencies across North America were reacting to Bowlby's report[2] to the World Health Organization, which demonstrated that institutional care for infants was potentially damaging to both their immediate and their long-term mental health. As a result, welfare agencies were making a determined effort to place children into foster or adoptive homes rather than institutions. The Neil McNeil Home remained the only agency in Toronto still providing institutional care for infants.

Shortage of Catholic foster and adoptive homes had created a situation by which this 50-year-old institution was seriously overcrowded, accommodating 85 children in a space adequate for only 50. Typically, infants who had been admitted in anticipation of early adoption had to remain in this sterile environment until they were approximately four years of age. By this time, their behaviour was sufficiently abnormal to preclude home placement. As a result, they proceeded to further institutional care – a great waste of human potential, and unfortunately, a situation re-enacted in similar institutions around the world.

---

1 Flint, B.M. (1959). *The security of infants*. Toronto: University of Toronto Press. Full report to be found in B.M. Flint (1978), *New hope for deprived infants*. Toronto: University of Toronto, Press.
2 Bowlby, J. (1952). *Maternal care and mental health*. Geneva: World Health Organization.

Phase I

Validity Study: 1956–57

Of these 85 children, a sample of 16 infants 3–24 months of age was selected to investigate the validity of a revised Flint Infant Security Scale. Its validity was confirmed. However, in human terms, the outlook for these infants was bleak. Each of the babies showed significant impairment in mental health. The more prolonged the institutional experience, the more severe was the effect. Our observations of this sample convinced us that our results could be generalized to all the children resident in this institution.

Original Assessment of the Infants and Their Environment: 1957–58

Several ameliorating factors emerged from our data which convinced us that, given a 'normalizing' environment, at least some of the babies could recover from their obvious emotional, social, and intellectual deficits. The first of these factors was the observation that, when first assessed at around three months of age, most of the babies were mentally healthy. However, by nine months and from there on to 24 months of age, mental health status deteriorated rapidly. The babies' early mental health suggested a potential capacity to respond favourably to a salutary environment. The second factor was a great range of individuality in the children's reactions to their depriving environment. There was a surprising difference in the security scores of children whose histories, physical well-being, length of time in the institution, and quality of caretaking were identical. For example, two such children showed a startling 43 points' difference between their mental health scores at the age of nine months. A third factor was the impact on all but three of the subjects of a routine move from one barren ward to another. This was demonstrated by a consistent drop in their mental health scores. This finding led to the speculation that, in the absence of significant attachment objects and caretakers on whom to focus, these children had formed their concept of self by relating to seemingly insignificant aspects of their environment. Hence, such things as a chip in the crib, a shadow on the wall, or a predictable squeak in the floor were vital to their sense of well-being. Removal of such referents created anxiety.

The general behaviour of the infants was bizarre. They were withdrawn from and disinterested in their world; further, their limp motor capabilities, grossly retarded development, and inability to relate to adults or peers precluded successful placement in whatever foster or adoptive homes were available. The Catholic Children's Aid had therefore developed a system of placement for such children in a series of institutions as they grew older. By the time many of these children reached the age of majority (18 years), they were unfit to function on their own when discharged from wardship. The accepted belief at this time was that such damage from the time of infancy was irreversible. However, bolstered by the conviction of the researchers that at least some of the children could be rescued, the Catholic Children's Aid and the research staff of the Institute of Child Study, University of Toronto undertook a partnership to establish a therapeutic environment in the Neil McNeil Home. The goal was to prepare the children for foster and adoptive homes.

The chief investigator, a member of the research staff at the Institute of Child Study, obtained grants over a period of years that enabled sweeping changes within the institution and later permitted follow-up studies on long-term outcomes for these children. Research was based on established age-appropriate behaviours along the maturational spectrum, and a security theory of mental health.

The challenges were daunting. The staff of the institution had failed to recognize that children acquire human strengths only when their childhood needs are acknowledged and met. A constant stream of impersonal, uncommunicative caretakers had moved through the children's lives, giving efficient but hurried routine care. As a result, no close warm relationships existed between the children and the adults. The environment, devoid of toys and offering no opportunity for the children's self-initiated action, resulted in apathetic and listless behaviour. Developmental assessment was thus impossible. The children as a group appeared grossly defective. During their waking hours they often remained in bed; they seldom left their own nursery, and almost never went outdoors. Life was drab. Nothing new or different entered their experience (except the changing of caretakers). Toilet training and eating routines for each child were the same regardless of age and readiness. No child was recognized as an individual with possessions or clothes of his or her own. Everything was shared, and those children capable of walking were herded about in groups on their rare emergence from their nurseries. Despite adequate nutrition, the children were emaciated, limp, and underweight. Although they had lived together since birth, they apparently derived no satisfaction from contact with each other, and no meaningful interaction took place between them. Speech was non-existent and vocalization infrequent. They seemed unable to conceive that social interactions might be rewarding. In fact, they were indifferent to all aspects of their environment.

Phase II

Modification of the Environment, Placement in Families, and Evaluation of Adaptation: 1958–78

The goal of phase II was to provide an environment that would move the children into the mainstream of normal development. The rehabilitative program, which lasted almost three years, gradually brought about dramatic changes in the children's behaviour. Thus, we were enabled, through time, to remove all 85 children from the institution to foster or adoptive homes.

In order to achieve this, the caretaking staff was doubled and trained in child development to meet the emotional, physical, and intellectual needs of the children. Staff and volunteers were assigned to individual children. Affectionate interaction between adults and children was encouraged; this would enable the children to be taken into the community with people they could trust. As well, the physical environment was changed: partitions between cribs and swaddled cribs, which had kept the children remote from stimulation as well as from playing with toys, were removed, and a deliberate program of stimulation through play and adult intervention began. The children's diet was modified to accommodate their level of development. Self-help was encouraged whenever the opportunity arose in dressing, eating, and toilet training. Clothing and toys, as well as beds and living quarters, were allocated to each child so that he or she might have something unique and personal with which to identify. Further, a deliberate attempt was made to encourage the use of language by labelling and identifying objects and activities.[3]

3 Flint, B.M. (1966). *The child and the institution: A study of deprivation and recovery.* Toronto: University of Toronto Press.

As the children gradually, and at their own pace, responded to stimulation, placement in homes became a feasible plan. Chapter 4 describes this process of recovery.

Thirty-one of the children in the therapeutic program (who by this time ranged in age from one year, seven months through five years, 11 months) were selected for an intensive follow-up study. They were placed in foster or adoptive homes when, as the result of the therapeutic program, (1) they were judged capable of relating to caregivers by displaying emotional depth (immature dependent trust), (2) they showed a capacity for constructive effort in play activity (self-directed effort), and (3) they exhibited an acceptable degree of mental health on the Flint Infant Security Scale and the Pre-school Mental Health Scale (Institute of Child Study, University of Toronto). These children and their families were readily available for follow-up interviews with the research and guidance worker. Three of the original 31 were lost from the study.

Information was regularly collected according to the following plan to acquire formal data (Table 1). The Stanford Binet Test of Intelligence (L–M) was administered at six, nine, and 12 years of age, to assess the intellectual functioning of the children. The Wechsler Intelligence Scale for Children (WISC) was used at age 15 only. The Rorschach Ink Blot Projective Test was used to explore the children's concept of their world. Each of these measures was used at ages six, nine, 12, and 15 years, with the exception of the Vineland Scale of Social Maturity. Information for the security measures was obtained from home interviews of parents and school interviews of teachers.

TABLE 1
Data collection for follow-up sample (*n*=31)

Data collected	Ages in years									
	6	7	8	9	10	11	12	13	14	15
Biannual interviews	X	X	X	X	X	X	X	X	X	X
School records	X	X	X	X	X	X	X	X	X	X
Security measures	X			X			X			X
Social maturity				X			X			X
Intelligence rating	X			X			X			X
Rorschach	X			X			X			X

A unique aspect of the families with whom the children were placed was the fact that most of the mothers were very stable emotionally, had been volunteers in the institution, and were prepared to take 'high-risk' children. All agreed to provide information for the research. All had a Christian value system, which was important to them. None were young. All the fathers had stable jobs and owned homes. With the exception of three families, all belonged to the lower socio-economic level of society, as defined by the Blishen Scale of Occupational Class (1958).

Nearly half the families were childless. Most of those women who had children remained at home in a traditional maternal role. Occasionally, mothers supplemented the family income with part-time jobs (only half the group did so).

Two of the children in the study subsequently lost an adoptive parent by death, and one by separation. Of the six children in foster homes (most of the children were adopted), three foster children had to be removed to institutional care and were later moved to group homes.

One of the unique aspects of this study was the continuity provided by the child care worker associated with it. As the director of the institutional therapeutic program, she became well acquainted with the children and highly concerned for their welfare. She was involved in their placement in homes and finally became the collector of data and the case worker for the remaining nine years of the study. Well steeped in the security theory of mental health and backed by the research team, who worked as consultants to support her efforts, she was able to establish a deeply trusting relationship with the families and their children, as was confirmed by parents' responses to a questionnaire in the final year of phase II. (This questionnaire appears in Appendix 2.)

By the time data collection was complete for every child, our group ranged in age from 15 through 18 years. Although systematic data collection was terminated by 15 years of age, casual contact was maintained with many of the families through the next few years.

A method of analysis was developed to ensure optimal use, not only of our test data, but also of our rich collection of case histories, which ranged from formal psychiatric progress notes to informal notations about family parties and noteworthy school events and achievements. Personal opinions of parents and teachers were omitted in favour of facts in the analysis.

The information from the records collected in home interviews was used in a variety of ways. Only statements that described the children's actual behaviour were used in analysis. Implicit in this analysis was the belief that recurring behaviour reflected the feeling states of the children. Analysis was carried out at ages six, nine, 12, and 15 years.

Behavioural statements were assigned to categories appropriate not only to the concepts of security, but also to the concepts of the Vineland Social Maturity Scale. Rorschach tests were analysed at ages six, nine, 12, and 15 years to identify the children's level of conceptual maturity. Intelligence tests (full scores and sub-scores) were examined according to the Binet and WISC Intelligence Scales for indications of changes in intellectual function.

It was hoped that the results of these analyses at 15 years of age would demonstrate the degree to which these children had overcome their early, severe developmental disabilities. It was assumed that our expectations regarding healthy adaptation would be confirmed if this group at age 15 (1) demonstrated trusting relationships with their families and other adults, (2) were motivated to learn both at school and in self-chosen activities, (3) demonstrated feelings of confidence in their approach to the challenges of their lives, and (4) were making use of their intellectual capacities.

Intellectual Functioning

The early intellectual development of the children had been so depressed as to be described as 'deficient intelligence, lack of affect, a dearth of drive and constructive behaviour and an almost complete inability to learn.' Although the therapeutic program within the institution had been designed to overcome such deviations, and later normal home and school environments were expected to enhance their intellectual abilities, it was anticipated that many of the children would still demonstrate impaired intellectual function at 15 years of age. Therefore, it was surprising to discover that the group as a whole measured within the average range of intelligence even by six years of age. A few low-functioning children seemed unable to achieve higher performance over time despite their normalizing environments, while others made great leaps in the level of intellectual function, some finally measuring in the superior level. It appeared that those children who had potential for intellectual growth responded to their new experiences with marked change while others possibly limited by genetic endowment, remained essentially unchanged. It appeared that the children's intellectual development, as marked by intelligence tests, showed more resilience and was more responsive to normalizing environment than any other aspect (social or emotional) of their development. One would speculate that conversely, it was probably also most vulnerable to deprivation experiences.

Other studies of children suffering early stimulus and social deprivation had reported a permanent weakness in verbal abilities. However, the children in our study showed unexpected strength in test items indicative of verbal reasoning and abstract skills. Also, there was a significant superiority in performance tasks over verbal ones at 15 years of age. Hence, it appeared that the overall functioning of our group of children had not been significantly depressed by their early experience. One of the most striking features of their performance when being tested was their consistently high level of motivation to participate in the tasks. This healthy characteristic was noted by the psychologist after the assessments at ages nine, 12, and 15 years.

Mental Health (Security)

Continuous analysis of the children's life data was undertaken, according to the concepts of security theory, in order to assess changes in mental health. Contrary to expectation, most of the children developed compatible relationships with their foster and adoptive families, and this promoted healthy psychological development. Starting by six years of age (with the exception of three foster children), they developed trust in their parents of a comfortably dependent nature, relying on them for care and direction. By the time they were between nine and 12 years of age, this relationship shifted to a more mature one that reflected continuing trust yet more self-direction and independent striving on the part of the children. By 15 years this progress had continued, but the children's relationships still suggested a dependence that might have been expected only of younger children. From six through 15 years of age they were highly effortful children, putting enthusiasm into their relationships and activities. By 15 years of age the group was described as highly motivated, immature, but mentally healthy.

Social Maturity

Life data on the children were examined to determine changes in level of social awareness and capabilities. Using the Vineland Social Maturity Scale, the data were analysed along two dimensions: personal care and social responsibility. It was assumed that social development moved from (1) dependence to independence, in terms of receiving personal care and developing competence through self-help, and (2) irresponsibility to responsibility, in the sense of becoming a contributing member of society in adulthood.

In these terms, the children consistently seemed younger than would be expected for their ages at nine, 12, and 15 years. By 15 years of age this immaturity approximated three years, i.e., the children at 15 years were socially more like 12-year-olds. This immaturity was increasingly evident from ages nine to 15 years, as though once a certain level was attained, further maturation slowed. In contrast, the children's intellectual achievements were consistently higher than their levels of social maturity.

These results raised the question of whether this social immaturity might indicate a permanent deficiency that could be attributed to the children's early lack of social awareness while institutionalized. Our analysis revealed that after placement, despite the children's ability to invest themselves deeply in family life, they had encountered consistent difficulty in peer relationships and were not ready for social responsibility. This conclusion was reinforced by the observation that few of these children had anything but casual involvement in group or community activities.

Concept Formation

Analysis of the Rorschach data at ages six, nine, 12, and 15 years was carried out on 10 children according to criteria established by Ames, Metraux, and Walker.[4] This was used to evaluate the children's emerging concepts about their world.

Although the Rorschach Ink Blot Projective Test was typically used to explore the nature of emotional reactions to one's world, the scheme of analysis developed by Ames et al. proved uniquely useful for our study. Focusing on adolescent age-appropriate characteristics, their study elaborated on the way in which an individual conceptualized the world. How did an individual impose meaning and order on experiences in order to make sense of them?

Assessed by these criteria, our children demonstrated a unique pattern of cognitive development. Unlike normal children, who display

4 Ames, L.B., Metraux, R.W., & Walker, R.N. (1971). *Adolescent Rorschach responses.* New York: Brunner/Mazel.

constricted and concrete thinking at six years of age and move to more diversity and complexity by age nine, our group showed a reversal of this pattern. The six-year-olds' diversity and complexity had a bizarre flavour, which was overcome by age nine with a return to more constricted and concrete thought characteristics that were anchored in reality. By 15 years, a healthy pattern of organization of conceptual function was continued, but the level of function more closely resembled that of a 12-year-old. At age 15, rather than demonstrate the expected age-appropriate tendencies toward reflection, introspection, and inactivity, our subjects displayed the activity and extroversion more characteristic of 12-year-olds, who react more impulsively to stimuli. While alert to external stimuli, our subjects seemed prone to participate at a superficial level without a corresponding engagement of emotional depth. Qualitatively, these children relied strongly on the structures of reality provided for them externally, rather than demonstrating a capacity to generate their own structures from their inner reflections.

More advanced complexity of thought, associated with increased awareness of deeper levels of meaning to experience, had not yet developed. This delay, in conjunction with the social immaturity of these children at 15 years, indicated a capacity to function appropriately in structured situations but a tendency to cope less maturely in situations requiring independent decisions, insight, and judgment. Despite this weakness and the early unusual pattern of development, the sequence of conceptual organization was, by age 15 years, in the mainstream of normalcy, although immature.

Phase III

Evaluation of the Subjects' Adaptation as Adults: 1988–93

Phase III was undertaken to address some of the unanswered questions that arose at the end of phase II. The subjects were then 28 to 31 years old. Given the cognitive delays at 15 years of age, one wondered:

- Would these subjects always need external systems for their orientation and direction? Might there be a permanent lack of imagination and capacity for reflection? Could they continue to monitor their expanding experiences, evaluate them, and adapt in order to achieve a greater subtlety of thought and an accompanying sophistication in behaviour?

- Would our subjects have replaced their immature dependency on their families with a more mature mode of functioning to become self-sufficient and independently functioning young adults?
- What events had characterized their emancipation from their families? Did this transition take place smoothly, with residual good feelings for both child and parents, or was there angry rebellion and resentment?
- Had the consistent difficulty with peer relationships been overcome, so that mutually supportive friendships might blossom and endure?
- What kind of parents might our subjects be? What would characterize their parenting styles? Would these subjects have developed a capacity to relate warmly and protectively to spouse and children?
- Were our early intellectual assessments predictive of our subjects' later success in education and the workforce? Did our subjects continue their high level of effortful activity throughout their early adult life?
- What would be our subjects' views of the world today and their place in it? Would they have maintained their early strong religious affiliations? Had they developed a philosophy to explain events and injustices to their own satisfaction?

In an attempt to answer some of these questions, it was determined that we would try to find our subjects, who were now mature adults, and interview them. A few had maintained contact with the case worker and were readily enlisted in the project. Others had disappeared from our lives and took considerable sleuthing to locate. However, 20 of the original 28 were located, and all agreed to participate.

Accordingly, when a research team was assembled, it included the case worker; a second member, who had worked intermittently on the earlier project; and a third, who was the original chief investigator. A questionnaire was developed based on the concepts of security theory, and was to be used as a guide for a free-flowing interview. This would explore the subjects' present relationships to parents, siblings, peers, spouse or partner, vocational adjustment, philosophy of life, and religious beliefs. Emotional well-being attitudes toward self, money, hobbies were also explored. (The interview format is given in Appendix 1.)

Interviews were arranged in the subjects' homes or at the Institute of Child Study and were conducted by one or another of the research team who was familiar with both security theory and the subjects' histories. The process of locating subjects, arranging meetings, and interviewing extended over several years.

When all the interviews were completed, the data were analysed according to the categories established in the interview format and then linked to the histories of the subjects. These were reported in the form of a developmental 'portrait.' The analysis of this longitudinal data proved painstaking and time consuming. As a result, reporting was not possible until 1993.

Study of a Contrast Group: 1989–92

As the final interviews with our subjects were concluding, it was determined that we would seek data on a contrast group that had shared common beginnings with our long-term subjects but who had been discharged to traditional foster care shortly after the therapeutic program began. The names of these children were available from our early institutional records.

These children would not have experienced the concentrated attention given our primary group, but rather would have been placed in foster homes under the supervision of agency workers who were then responsible for monitoring their progress. Each child's history would be recorded by the case worker assigned to him or her. There would be information about the child's relationship to the foster family, perhaps to the biological family, and to peers, as well as the child's adaptation to school and community. These records would track each child's progress and would be used also for planning in times of transition or crisis.

These records were retrieved from microfiche data in the archives of the CCAS.

2

Security and Mental Health

The goal of our longitudinal study, from the children's early institutionalization to their later adaptation to home, school, and community, had been to find ways to relieve the effects of their early deprivation and promote their mental health. If this goal were successful, we believed the children would be capable of dealing with life's challenges. To provide a focus for our intervention, the conceptual framework of security theory, as elaborated by W.E. Blatz,[1] was adopted. Dr Blatz had described his framework as a 'system to clarify human potential' and elaborated it most fully for the adult years. Flint[2] and colleagues modified this theory to be more appropriate for infancy and the pre-school years. As our study progressed, further modifications were made to describe the transitions from school age through adolescence.

Security Theory

Dr Blatz believed that every individual, young or old, was engaged in the achievement of a feeling of security or serenity. He believed that the constant striving to achieve this state was a dynamic and never-ending journey that involved an individual in a constant stream of choices throughout the lifespan. A mentally healthy person presented with a problem experiences anxiety which he or she relieves by making a conscious decision.

Having made a decision, one can accept its consequences with equanimity and hence achieve a feeling of serenity. Depending on the cir-

---

1 Blatz, W.E. (1966). *Human security*. Toronto: University of Toronto Press.
2 Flint, B.M. (1959). *The security of infants*. Toronto: University of Toronto Press.

cumstances, which can vary in gravity from choosing a mate to selecting peas or carrots for dinner, either a short-term or long-term sense of serenity is achieved. An adult who has developed a habit of making decisions enjoys a state of mind that welcomes challenges and accepts insecurity as part of living.

When faced with a problem an individual can make decisions in a variety of ways, some of which are healthier than others. These decisions are an integral part of all aspects of life, and can involve relationships, vocation, avocation, and philosophy (including religion). One healthy method of decision making is to put forth effort to acquire knowledge and skills, thereby relying on oneself to make a decision and to accept the consequences of it. Thus, one is acting in an *independently secure* manner. A second and equally healthy way to solve problems is to enlist the knowledge and skills of another who shares the decision making and its consequences. Usually, this person is a peer with whom one has developed a *mature dependency*. These individuals are involved in an interdependent relationship.

Another, less healthy, way of making decisions is to rely on a more knowledgeable or skilled individual to solve one's problems and to accept consequences for decisions. This regressive approach is similar to that of a very young child and is an expression of an *immature dependent* relationship. With this method, one avoids making decisions and accepting consequences but is left vulnerable in two ways: (1) one gets little practice in decision making to solve problems, and (2) the individual on whom one relies may not always be available. A fourth and potentially unhealthy way of problem solving is to avoid making decisions (as in procrastination) and hence having to accept responsibility. This approach makes use of *deputy agents* or strategies that provide a temporary sense of security. In a very young child, these may manifest in a wide variety of defensive behaviours – crying, refusal of offers of affection, clinging, rejection of food, hyperactivity, scattered attention, and apathy. Such deputy agents may vary in nature, intensity, and persistence at any given time from infancy into adulthood. While they are adopted to relieve anxiety, they in fact prolong it because they do not help to resolve underlying problems.

The maturing individual gradually selects more successful deputy agents for solving problems through expending effort. In addition, he or she increasingly limits defences to those that have been most effective in achieving goals. These might include lying, cheating, avoiding, procrastinating, blaming others, using excuses, using flattery, and many other strategies, which become 'crutches' to lean on in times of crisis. In the adult, these strategies, may manifest in such defences as 'sour grapes' ('who cares?'), denial ('not me'), rationalization ('only an idiot would do that'), compensation ('at least I have money'), and sublimation ('work hard to forget it').

In a mentally healthy person, temporary use of deputy agents is acceptable to defer difficult decision making until a more adequate solution to a problem is found. A mentally healthy adult remains aware that he or she is using defences. However, there is potential danger that their habitual use might result in loss of insight, in which case one slips across the line from good to poor mental health. When particular deputy agent mechanisms become entrenched ways of avoiding reality, a person is deemed ill. Mental illness is not a definable syndrome, but rather a continuum expressing degree of health or lack of it. In more severe illness, deputy agents may be evident as obsessive-compulsive behaviour, hysteria, and paranoia.

Conceptual Framework

For our study, in order to provide a psychological framework for both research and guidance procedures, we had to elaborate upon the concept of security developmentally, from infancy to maturity. An emphasis on decision making and independence would be inappropriate for an infant. Therefore it was necessary to ask the question, 'What kinds of experience in infancy and early childhood lead to the capacity to make decisions and accept responsibility in adulthood?'

At the beginning of an infant's life, it is impossible to divorce the well-being of the child from the care provided by the mother. The quality of this first relationship is critical to the mental health of the very young. Any understanding of an infant's feeling of security is entwined with the nature of the caretaking he or she receives. Hence, the following conceptual framework was adopted.[3]

From birth throughout infancy, mental health depends on the development of an immature dependent relationship through which a mother provides consistent, dependable attention to an infant's needs. Through sensitive caretaking, healthy feelings are generated which reflect an infant's warm feeling of dependent trust in the world and good feelings of self-trust (confidence). Hence, from consistent, dependable

3 Flint, B.M. (1959). *The security of infants.* Toronto: University of Toronto Press.

need reduction, an infant gradually learns to anticipate relief from insecurity and discomfort, and begins to associate this with the mother on whom he or she has learned to depend. A child who experiences this association can be described as being in a state of *immature dependent security*, the first step in a developmental sequence of healthy adjustment. The second step in this sequence emerges as a child internalizes the feeling that recurring states of discomfort will undoubtedly be relieved. He or she now begins to anticipate that needs will generally be met, that discomfort is transitory, and that the world is a benign place. Such trust in a dependable world allows the child the comfort of expressing both positive and negative feelings without fear of rejection. This trust encourages the expression of effort and frees an infant to explore the world.

This state of *dependent trust* extends throughout the child's later development and becomes increasingly flavoured with feelings of competence and self-reliance. As a child grows in competence to deal with daily problems, he or she gradually relinquishes reliance on the parent as an agent for activity and as a buffer against the consequences of it, and increasingly depends on self-initiated effort to solve problems. Such self-rewarding activity further enables the child to accept the consequences of his or her behaviour, increasingly set personal goals, admit mistakes, and tolerate criticism. This confidence that one is a worthy individual is termed *self-worth*.

A child moving from infancy to maturity experiences a mixture of the three psychological states described as immature dependence, dependent trust, and self-worth, and his or her mental health reflects the balance of these states.[4] It is our belief that the balance shifts from infancy to maturity in the direction of less immature dependency toward increased dependent trust and self-worth. Furthermore, we believe the shift in balance among these psychological states to be reflected in maturing behaviour as the child interacts with persons and objects in the world. As children mature, many changes take place in the relationship between parent and child. Increasing internalization of children's secure feelings is reflected in emerging competencies, self-confidence, and effort. We know that a child generates and maintains immature dependence on caretakers from early infancy through to maturity; we also know that this reliance decreases through

---

4 Flint, B.M. (1978). *New hope for deprived children.* Toronto: University of Toronto Press.

time. What we do *not* know is the point at which this quality changes to the kind of relationship that we have chosen to call dependent trust. The quality of dependent trust replaces in large part the necessity for immature dependency, while still allowing the child to continue a comfortable reliance on caretakers. Whereas immature dependency has been characterized by immediate need for physical assistance and specific directives about behaviour, dependent trust is characterized by the child's internalizing the values of the parents, hence reducing the need for constant supervision. Now the child has begun to shift the relationship to the more mature form of functioning.

A relationship of dependent trust implies less leaning upon the directives of one's parents, accompanied by more independent action, which arises from the confidence that one's activities and feelings will largely be supported and approved by one's parents. Such a relationship cannot take place until sufficient of the parental values have been internalized that the child can function within a frame of reference that is relatively congenial to that of the family. When this state of mind has been achieved, the child now derives emotional support from three factors: (1) through feelings of compatibility with the parents and their goals for the child; (2) through reliance on the internalized parental values; and (3) through increasingly self-directed activity. Such an achievement does not preclude the possibility that the child is putting forth effort, particularly in peer relationships, that may not harmonize with all parental values. It does imply that much of this self-directed activity will be congenial to the parents. Hence, we find children with well-internalized dependent trust carrying sufficient feelings of confidence that they can both accept and question the nature of parental controls.

Because *effortful behaviour* is a demonstrable part of a healthy personality, it is therefore an integral part of security theory from infancy through maturity. Throughout a child's life, it is associated with feeling states of both immature dependence and dependent trust; it develops out of the first relationship that infants form with their mother when they learn, through her care and consistency, that they are living in a dependable, predictable, and comfortable world. Such predictability allows children to define the limits of their world and to interpret the meaning of their experiences. The mother's interest demonstrates, furthermore, that the child is a person of worth. Such feelings of self-worth are attended by confidence and curiosity, and produce a child who is self-directed in exploring the world, both in its social and material aspects. As the child's relationship with the parents changes from immature dependence to dependent trust, effortful behaviour continues to be associated with both. Dependent trust allows children to feel that their efforts will largely be supported by their caretakers, and gives them the 'go ahead' to become increasingly self-directed in peer relationships, school activities, and family and community living.

The states of immature dependence and dependent trust provide the foundation for later mature dependent security in adulthood, while effort is the greatest component of later independent security.

Table 2 summarizes the feelings associated with security from infancy to adulthood.

The security model of mental health was a useful framework from which to shape a recovery program for our young subjects. This same model was adopted as the basis for our interviews with our adult subjects. Intimacies (extra-familial and familial), vocation (school and work), avocation (hobbies), and philosophy (religion, use of money, sense of justice and social responsibility) were explored according to a systematic format. Although the interviews were highly individual for each subject, care was taken to cover all aspects of the security model.

Such a model would not be appropriate for all cultures, for example, in cultures that discourage individualism in favour of dependence on the group. However, this model was believed to be a valid one for the Western culture represented by our subjects and their society.

Summary

Good mental health is developed in infancy through a solid relationship built on dependent trust between caretaker and child. Through this relationship children gain confidence to put forth effort to explore their environment. Throughout the pre-school and elementary school years, continuing mental health is expressed in the consolidation of coexisting feelings of dependent trust and self-trust.

In middle childhood and pre-adolescence, a child becomes increasingly more competent to deal with the world, make decisions, and accept the consequences of those decisions and actions. At the same time, parents are increasingly unable to anticipate children's needs and reduce their anxiety. Hence, a healthy child increases self-directed effort. The consequences of such activity are self-reinforcing, leading to greater confidence and further effort. At this stage, the interaction between parent and child continues to shift from immature dependence

TABLE 2
Feelings associated with security from infancy to adulthood

Characteristics of good mental health

Developmental stage

Infancy
- A sense of dependent trust that one's needs will always be met by sensitive, caring adults (usually mother)
- A feeling that the world is benign
- A sense of self-worth which gives the confidence to put forth effort in the exploration of one's world

Childhood
- Comfortable acceptance and internalization of most family values
- Pursuit of self-directed goals, with the expectation that most will find parental support
- A sense of control over one's own goals and enjoyment of effort in all aspects of life — school, hobbies, work, friendships, and family life

Adulthood
- An ability to make independent decisions and accept the consequences with equanimity
- A capacity to establish a mature reciprocal relationship with another person with whom one shares decisions and consequences
- A sense that expenditure of effort toward self-chosen goals is worthwhile

---

Characteristics of poor mental health

Infancy
- A sense of uncertainty that one's needs will be met, resulting from inconsistency or ambivalence on the part of caretakers
- Hesitancy to expend effort in tasks and social relations because it may not always be rewarded by caretakers

Childhood
- An inability to accept and internalize sufficient family values to be trusted by one's parents
- Feelings of anxiety about the pursuit of self-directed goals and hence, erratic expenditure of effort
- Use of compensatory regressive and deputy-agent mechanisms to mask insecurity resulting in overly aggressive or withdrawn behaviour.

Adulthood
- An inability to make decisions and accept their consequences
- An all-pervasive anxiety, which can be allayed for a short while by the use of regressive or deputy-agent mechanisms
- A permanent reliance on pervasive deputy agents or regression, accompanied by little insight into their use.

(reliance on physical care and parental directives) to increased dependent trust, with the child demonstrating increased self-reliance. If
the child has internalized sufficient of the family's values to ensure
their support for his efforts, the transition is more likely to be a smooth
one.

By adulthood, a mentally healthy person becomes assured of his or
her own values and has the confidence to make independent choices
in life. This ability to make decisions and solve problems promotes a
sense of security or serenity.

3

Unique Developmental Patterns: A Key to Therapeutic Intevention

In planning therapeutic interventions for these institutionalized children, we used the term 'therapy' in a specific, though non-traditional, sense. Therapy was regarded as the provision of a healing atmosphere of acceptance for each child as a unique individual, whose best capabilities and characteristics could unfold under the nurturance of committed caretakers. Such caretakers would require knowledge about normal developmental patterns and would understand the needs of very young children for consistent, affectionate parenting, for selective attachments, for cognitive stimulation, and for kindly direction and discipline.

Thus, staff needed to be recruited and trained, who could translate such knowledge into practice. Two themes formed the core of staff training. The first was security theory, which (as discussed in Chapter 2) emphasizes on the quality of caretaker–child relationships and the shift to dependent trust that needs to occur as children mature. The second theme was the variability in developmental patterns shown by children as they mature. For example, at the same chronological age, a group of children will display divergent levels of cognitive, motor, social, and emotional competencies and characteristics.

Variability in Development

A few children could be termed 'even developers,' showing similar levels in all four aspects of development when examined against chronological age (c.a.), e.g.:

C.A.	*10 months*
Cognitive	11 months
Motor	10 months
Emotional	10 months
Social	11 months

Other children might show considerable unevenness:

C.A.	*10 months*
Cognitive	12 months
Motor	8 months
Emotional	12 months
Social	8 months

or:

C.A.	*10 months*
Cognitive	7 months
Motor	10 months
Emotional	8 months
Social	7 months

Such divergent patterns might be observed among children in a given age group. As well, the rate at which these patterns emerged might vary for an individual child over time. For example, one child's development from eight to 12 months of age might keep pace with her chronological age in an even fashion:

	Months					
Chronological Age	8	9	10	11	12	
Developmental Age	8	9	9	10	12	(average)

However, another child might proceed in 'spurts and starts' compared with his C.A.:

	Months				
Chronological Age	8	9	10	11	12
Developmental Age	8	8	9	12	12

Another variation in pattern might be observable when comparing, over time, one facet of a child's development with another:

	Months				
Chronological Age	8	9	10	11	12
Cognitive	8	8	8	10	11
Motor	6	6	8	8	9
Emotional	7	8	8	9	9
Social	7	8	8	9	10

With such variability in mind, we initiated rehabilitative measures within the institution (as described in Chapter 1) and attempted to chart each child's progress on a monthly basis. Much to our surprise, many months passed before we were able to make any developmental evaluations at all on these passive and unresponsive children. Gradually, as each child showed some response to the new program, we realized that not only was there a great and generalized developmental delay, but also there was unusual unevenness among the various aspects of each child's development. Eventually, we stopped using chronological age as a yardstick of development in favour of the term 'developmental age.'

Another characteristic that distinguished our subjects from normal children was their predisposition to progress in only one or two aspects of development while lagging in others. The staff often speculated that a child could concentrate on only one or two aspects at a time. Hence, growth in social and emotional development might proceed at the expense of cognitive and motor abilities or vice versa.

As each child responded individually to the rehabilitative measures, some of this observed unevenness in development abated. Eventually, behaviours appeared that were sufficiently 'normal' to warrant foster or adoptive placement. The four criteria used to reach this decision were: (1) evidence of dependent trust in caretakers, (2) capacity to use intelligence by acting upon the play environment in a competent and reality-oriented way, (3) evidence of relating playfully to peers, and (4) pride in efforts toward self-help in such activities as dressing, eating, and toileting.

Regression

Although the children could demonstrate developmentally appropriate behaviour in the institution, we were aware that the stress of adapting to home life might create confusion, resulting in disorganization and regression. However, we could not predict in what areas (e.g., coping, functioning, or adapting) regression might be evident. Most placements were preceded by several home visits to cushion the impact for parents as well as children and to allow everyone to anticipate the reality of the transition to a new way of life.

After placement, it became evident that sufficient socialization had taken place during treatment that most of the children passed adequately through the traditional 'honeymoon' period, that is, they conformed to the expectations of their new parents and behaved pleasantly toward them. However, many children developed overwhelming tension as they tried to sense what was expected of them. As this period was negotiated, the gaps in their function became apparent once more. Some children had difficulty understanding the role of 'father' in a household and could relate comfortably only to a 'mother.' The relationships of husband to wife and of child to siblings were also difficult to grasp. Many of the casual interactions that are taken for granted in a normal household were misunderstood by our subjects. For example, when told to 'go to the kitchen and fetch me a glass of water,' a willing child grasped the significance of everything except the word 'fetch' and stood confused in the kitchen, unable to do anything more. Another child interpreted the warning 'Watch out!' as having something to do with a wrist watch. Other behaviour was simply regressive, as when a gangling five-year-old wanted to be rocked on his mother's lap before sleep.

To reduce the difficulties of this transition, many parents had to lower their expectations to meet the needs of such immature and unevenly developed children. In retrospect, we recognized that any child in transition from one cultural or family milieu to another (e.g., from an impoverished environment to a middle-class home or school) might display such behaviours.

Temperamental Orientation

As we kept monthly records on each child's progress within the institution, we became sensitive to individual children's approach to experiences. A guiding theory for therapy unfolded, which we used in determining how to interact with each child. We categorized the children loosely into three groups or types, according to temperamental orientation. While all the children exhibited characteristics of more than one orientation, most expressed one more strongly than the other two.

Type 1 children demonstrated a highly social orientation and seemed more sensitively attuned to the attention of caretakers than to play materials or events around them. Thus, the therapeutic approach for these children involved direct effort to build an initial trusting relationship by body contact, face-to-face conversation, and social reinforcement. Such children seemed most open to building a trusting relationship within a relatively short period of time and responded quickly to the therapy program as a whole.

Type 2 children tended to rebuff direct social rapport. They preferred to allow relationships to develop with adults through joint use of play materials and praise for efforts toward self-help. These children took longer to develop trusting relationships with staff, but eventually achieved this first step toward mental health.

Type 3 children seemed unresponsive to adults and play materials alike. However, cognitive activity seemed to be constant. Such children might be termed 'watchers': they often stationed themselves at a distance from the mainstream of activity, yet watched intently and ignored attempts to involve them. These children were hard to 'read' and were the most resistant to rehabilitative measures. Staff had to await some initial gesture indicating willingness to be involved, and the formation of trusting relationships thus took a long time. These children approached all new situations with great caution.

The goal of the institution's staff was to build each child's self-esteem by identifying each child's strengths and directing effort toward their enhancement. Weaknesses were minimized in the belief that they would diminish once personality and functional assets began to predominate. Hence, the sociable child received direct social support from adults and plenty of opportunity for cooperative peer interaction. The child who was oriented toward 'things' was provided with a material environment geared to capture interest; staff acted as mediators to reinforce such interest, indirectly demonstrating that adults could be trustworthy and dependable supports. 'Watchers' were exposed to consistent, reliable routines that encouraged trust because of their predictability; these children were not pressured to participate or interact. As they gained a sense of security and control, they demonstrated an ability to deal with new events and tolerate some intrusion of adults into their daily life. Following are descriptions of some children and their temperamental orientations.

Jane

Jane was a socially oriented child. Born prematurely, she weighed three pounds, 14 ounces at birth, and spent the first six weeks of her life in the Hospital for Sick Children in Toronto. On discharge she went directly to the institution. There she remained in a seriously underdeveloped state until the rehabilitation program began when she was three years, three months old. Although exhibiting many physical symptoms and general social unresponsiveness, she gradually was able to benefit from increased attention and deliberate stimulation. Eventually she was placed in a foster family when she was four years, seven months of age. This family of nine children, ranging in age from five to 24 years, was to become 'her only family,' where she remained until she completed her education. This large family could not afford to adopt Jane, and it was not until she reached adulthood that she assumed the family name.

As a child, Jane appeared to function within a dull-normal range on intellectual assessments, and this was generally reflected in her school achievement. However, her remarkable drive to achieve her own goals, which often appeared beyond her capabilities, enabled her to go beyond the aspirations and expectations of her foster family. As a young adult, she earned sufficient money to pay for training and eventually became a nursing assistant, where her kindness and sincerity were decided assets. She worked for seven years, confident in her nursing skills and coping well with responsibility. Because she 'found it too hard to watch the little ones suffer,' she chose geriatric nursing, which she enjoyed. Her career continued for two and a half years after her marriage, until she took maternity leave to have her first child. Now the mother of three pre-school children, she had not returned to hospital work, but acted as a substitute nursing assistant in a doctor's office. Her home, her three daughters (ages six months, two years, and five years) and her husband filled her time. She was a skilled homemaker: she baked, sewed, decorated her house, and guided her children's development in a thoughtful way, and with apparent ease.

Jane's relationship with her husband and children seemed unselfconsciously accommodating. This was evident as she welcomed the research team with a delicious lunch, in which her husband and two oldest children were included. The children spontaneously participated in the conversation. Her five-year-old read a story aloud. Jane gave the impression that nothing was too much effort. Her children were clean and charmingly dressed. Her home was well kept, and she was a gracious host.

She and her husband had been married eight years and seemed to share a steady, mature, loving relationship in which they supported each other. Jane said, 'I like him the way he is. If I get angry, he tries to calm me down.' They seemed to communicate well and showed a willingness to adapt to each other. 'If I annoyed him, he'd confront me with it and I'd try not to do it again.' It appeared that Jane had been fortunate to find a husband who respected her desire to please and do well, and reciprocated in kind. They shared the household chores and the care of the children. Favourite family activities included skating and tobogganing, walking, and talking. Jane was on good terms with her in-laws. 'I think they think I am pretty good. They are really good people. I couldn't have picked better ones.'

Jane had fond memories of her foster parents, both of whom had died within the previous five years. They made her feel part of their family, despite having little time for individual attention in such a large group, and despite their inability to adopt her because of financial constraints. She shared a satisfying relationship with her eldest foster sister, who was then 40. This sister had as large a family as her parents: four children born to her, one adopted, and six fostered. Jane's family often exchanged visits with her sister's family.

As well as close family ties, Jane also had both long-standing and new friends. One of her closest friends was a girl whom she had met in Grade 4 and with whom she had shared many joyous events, such as graduation. She maintained friends from her nursing days, and was active in her community. Eager to attend a party with their new neighbours when she and her husband first moved into their house, she said, 'We had a riot. I had them in stitches.'

Jane and her husband were capable in the management of money. As a child, she always spent her allowance carefully, and by age 13, she was able to save money for special plans. Her careful habits had continued into adulthood: she and her husband had no outstanding bills; they owned a car; their house was half paid for; they never went on spending sprees; and their credit card payments were dealt with promptly. Neither had ever received unemployment insurance or welfare, and they had 'never run out of money.' Jane said, 'There is nothing we really need.'

Jane's foster family was strongly religious. She had attended church and Catholic school, and she still attended mass. However, family unity took precedence over church affiliations, so she and her husband chose to have their daughters baptized in the Anglican faith. She seemed comfortable with this decision, and appeared to have no guilt or anxiety about it. She had rejected the Catholic church's stand on birth control and other issues. She and her husband agreed on religious matters. Jane felt that her concept of a just God had helped her overcome difficulties. Her religious faith, her reliance on her husband, and her protectiveness of her family had given meaning to her life.

Jane's world clearly revolved around her husband and children. Her earlier determination to train as a nursing assistant was mirrored in her present determination to protect and nurture her family. Her nursing career was insurance against future emergencies. Her adaptation to life, as characterized by her skills in accommodating, serving, and negotiating, seemed to have sprung from an innate loving nature.

Jane had survived the disadvantage of premature birth and the psychological isolation of subsequent hospitalization. She overcame the emotional and developmental deficits of early institutional living, and related successfully to an unusually large foster family. She had developed admirable homemaking skills, which served her young family well. She enjoyed life with her husband and children. In adulthood, Jane seemed to have retained the social orientation that characterized her as a child.

Maurice

Maurice was a child whose initial interest in his environment focused on material 'things' rather than social interactions. Reared in the institution from birth, he was apathetic and retarded at the beginning of the rehabilitation program. Through 'goal-corrected' activity – in which caretakers involved him in play with toys, and in dressing, feeding, and bathing – he was gradually able to accept and rely on trustworthy caretakers. By two years of age, he seemed to have a capacity to relate to caring adults, and showed average development upon intellectual assessment. He seemed ready for an adoptive home.

After placement – at age four years, two months – it became evident that Maurice's trust in adults had frail beginnings. Despite the dedication of his adoptive parents to consolidate their relationship with him, his first years were marked by recurring anxiety that he might lose them. A persistent inadequacy in peer relationships characterized his school and early adolescent years, a weakness compensated for by his remarkable mechanical skills. By high school, his capabilities in electronics elevated his status among his peers, boosting his self-worth and enabling him to bridge some of the gaps in his social skills.

Maurice's history demonstrates how particular skills can serve as a foundation on which to build secure feelings, which eventually permit the emergence of a comfortable sense of self. However, this is a long-term process. Maurice was placed in foster care, with a loving, older couple of Irish heritage (after 17 years of childless marriage). No effort was too great for these parents to help him adapt to their home and family. Legal adoption followed a year later. However, it became apparent, through his recurring bouts of disturbing behaviour, that he was a highly volatile, emotional child.

Maurice's chronic concern that he might lose his family created generalized anxiety, which erupted in sporadic incidents. For the most part, these episodes were allayed by his case worker's intervention. However, early in his school career, a teacher's religious discussion about death precipitated a serious, prolonged emotional upheaval that required psychotherapy. Despite this intervention, Maurice continued to tell his parents he loved them 10 or 12 times a day; he also feared their criticism. Eventually, he gained enough confidence to be able to accept anger in others and in himself. However, his underlying anxiety continued to the extent that even by 11 years of age, he was considered by parents, teacher, and case worker to be 'too helpful for a boy' and a 'perfectionist.'

During his school years, Maurice's persistent social immaturity among peers was a chronic matter of concern to his parents and to his case worker. His bossiness and insistence on having his own way led to his rejection by individual playmates. His disruptive intrusion into play groups usually created hostility. As a result, during his first two years at school he was isolated, both in the classroom and on the playground. Teachers and parents struggled with strategies to heighten his sensitivity to his classmates, but with little success. By the time he was 15 years of age, his social life was extremely limited, and he appeared to have given up any attempt to make friends.

Fortunately, and with the encouragement of his parents and case worker, Maurice began to develop solitary skills. He had always demonstrated average or above average intellectual abilities in test situations, though this was not borne out by his school performance. After the family's move to a small northern community where they had many relatives, Maurice's budding interest in carpentry and electricity was encouraged by his father. By age 10 he had built a tree house, a book-case, and a roll-up blind. By 11 years of age, he was taking electrical projects to school. At age 13, he took apart old radios and clocks and repaired them; he experimented with a tape recorder, bought electri-cal gadgets, and wired his parents' house. By 14, he was top electronics student in his regional high school. He developed a stimulating friend-ship with an older cousin who was taking electronic engineering. He was hired by a small museum to help with electrical work and plumb-ing, a job that also led to an interest in antiques. He helped his father build a cottage. Encouraged by their case worker, Maurice's parents arranged to have him apprenticed to a local repair man. This helped extend his social contacts and improved his communication skills. Eventually, he joined a basketball team in school, played floor hockey, and seemed to have made a few friends.

Thus, by 15 years of age, when phase II of our study was complete, Maurice had developed a deep and rewarding relationship with his nuclear family, a clearly defined direction for his interests, and practi-cal skills on which he could rely to entertain himself. There remained some question about his capacity to reach out for affectionate rela-tionships beyond his family. He no longer seemed lonely, but rather had learned to live comfortably without an extended social life. Based on his early emergent mechanical skills, it was predicted that 'he was likely to become a productive, self-supporting, and contributing mem-ber of his community.'[1]

Maurice was interviewed when he was 27 years of age. He welcomed the interviewing team to his home, which he was renovating. He served coffee cake of his own baking on his best china, and proudly dis-played his antique kitchen furniture and pictures of his cottage and his relatives.

Though deeply attached to his family, Maurice had been able to form sufficient friendships to support his leaving home after high school graduation at 19 years of age. He attended a community college 200 miles away, along with some friends from high school. On com-pletion of his course in electronics, he took a job near his friends in the city where he had attended college.

When he was 23 years old, Maurice was dealt a devastating double blow: both parents died unexpectedly, and within a week of each other.

1 Flint, B.M. (1978). *New hope for deprived children*. Toronto: University of Toronto Press.

Maurice was the only person in his extended family available to take responsibility for settling the estate. He resigned from his job and moved back home to settle his parents' affairs – a challenge he faced with little assistance from others. ('You'd think my aunts would have invited me to dinner once.') A year later, he sold the house ('two garage sales and 10 loads to the dump') and moved to the family cottage, where he lived alone for two years. Although not without some emotional crises, Maurice emerged from the experience of his parents' death a surprisingly stable young man. His statement that 'he had no choice' indicated his ability to take life's events in stride.

By age 27, Maurice seemed to have consolidated a sense of self, partly based on his identification with his adopted family and their values. His lack of success in obtaining information about his natural parents released him emotionally to relate wholeheartedly to his adoptive family's Irish and French heritage. During the interview, Maurice spoke warmly of his late adoptive parents and affectionately of his 103-year-old grandmother: 'She talks fast. I have to keep up my French for her. She's pretty active.' He pointed out, with pride, an attractive grouping of framed portraits of his parents, grandmother, aunts, and uncles, and also mentioned that he had assembled a family tree of his adoptive family. Although he expressed disappointment that he received little support from these relatives when his parents died, he still felt they were connected as a family by good memories and good times at the cottage.

Maurice's early mechanical interest shaped both his vocational and avocational skills, and provided him with a flexible trade that gave him confidence. Activities that had set him apart as a schoolboy seemed to have become the key to his work, his leisure, and his social life at age 27. While at college he excelled at computer hardware, and on graduation was employed testing computer parts for Amtrak and Via Rail. This job lasted only six months because of his parents' death. Later, after Maurice had moved to his cottage, he earned money doing electrical work for neighbours for a period of two years. Although he enjoyed being his own boss, he returned to the city where he still had friends, bought a house, and worked as a 'handyman.' He renovated his house and also helped his friends with remodelling projects, exchanging his electrical and plumbing expertise for his friends' skills, such as repairing his truck. Thus, his skills served not only to make him independent financially, but were also a source of interdependence with others.

At the time of the interview, Maurice did not have a job. His unemployment insurance had run out, but he did not need money. He had filed job applications with several firms, and expected to be hired when economic conditions improved. He seemed to have little concern about this aspect of his life, confident in his ability to work independently.

Thus by age 27, Maurice, although still a somewhat solitary individual, had extended his peer relationships far beyond what was anticipated for him at age 15. He still did not enjoy competitive sports, had a minor interest in skating and skiing, lived alone, borrowed books from the local library, and always had a home renovation project under way. He enjoyed going for walks by himself. He had attended an Irish Club in his neighbourhood and had proudly unearthed some 78 rpm Irish records at a rummage sale. Although he took comfort in his family's Irish heritage, Maurice had only minimal contact with his extended family. His solitary life seemed orderly and under his control. He had lost his early compulsive tidiness, regularly visited the doctor and dentist, and consciously kept himself healthy.

He had managed his inheritance well: he had kept the family cottage, and bought a small house and a van. He was a careful buyer, knowing where to get bargains. Although he used a credit card, he promptly paid his debts each month. Asked what he would do if he won a million dollars, he replied that he 'would have to give it away.'

One source of strength to Maurice was his Catholic faith. He enjoyed attending church every week because it made him 'feel closer to [his] maker.' He felt that God and religion 'pulled him through' when his parents died, and that God watched over his grandmother. He reasoned that positive and negative events 'balanced out' in this life and the next. For himself, he believed he had already coped with the worst possible tragedy – 'things can only go up.' Nuclear war did not worry him. The worst thing he could imagine was losing an arm. He was superstitious, admitting that he would avoid the numbers '13, 9, 7, or 3,' and that he watched out for black cats and 'Friday the thirteenth.'

The portrait of Maurice at age 27 is that of a relatively healthy young man. Still possessed of the sense of humour that was observed in him during childhood, he had a knack for telling droll stories and could laugh at himself. This young adult seemed to have developed a strong self-concept, largely based on his identification with his nuclear family. Although he had developed some mature dependencies with friends, he had yet to take the next step, by forming an intimate relationship with a partner. His lack of concern about needing a job may have reflected a true confidence in his technical skills, which indeed seemed the organizing principle for his personality.

Comparing Maurice's mental health at age 27 with that at age 15 led to the conclusion that he is in better health than one might have predicted and that he would likely continue to function in a healthy way in the future.

George

George, a 'watcher,' was three years and two months of age when the rehabilitation program began. His prior history, although sparse, indicated that he was a child who had considerable emotional resilience and basic alertness. These qualities doubtless helped him withstand social and stimulus deprivation for at least the first nine months of his life. However, by 18 months, deprivation was seen to be taking its toll. His development was lagging; he was 'fearful and lacking confidence.' Although interested in observing things around him, he was afraid to act, and would venture nowhere with an unfamiliar adult. In his first three years of life, George suffered many illnesses and even one hospitalization.

When first observed by the new staff, George was a compulsive, ritualistic child who lacked trust in adults, was unable to tolerate interference, and frequently screamed and had temper tantrums when approached. He was apprehensive of anything unfamiliar, was indifferent to playthings, and appeared passive and withdrawn much of the time. While sucking his thumb, he watched the nursery activity from a distance.

Placed in a small unit with five other children and a loving housemother who kept to a consistent routine, George gradually began to respond to the new program. His droopy physical posture straightened, his blank facial expression disappeared, and he began to display the healthy temperamental characteristics that would form his personality in future years.

The first healthy trait to appear was his capacity to relate to his caretakers and eventually develop a trusting attachment to them. A second trait was his heartening curiosity about the world around him, once he established that his world was safe.

For example, a picnic planned by the institution staff was eagerly anticipated by most of the children, despite their uncertainty as to the meaning of this first picnic in their lives. When the day arrived, most the children surged eagerly toward the waiting taxis. George, contra-rily, collapsed kicking and screaming on the doorstep and was finally carried, sobbing, to the taxi by his concerned housemother. Once at the picnic, however, he began slowly to participate in the activities until, caught up by the pleasure of it, his exuberance spilled over to affect everyone.

After 15 months of treatment, George's personality assets seemed to outweigh his disabilities, and an adoptive family was found for him. The planning for his adoptive placement was undertaken with his par-ticular qualities in mind. To overcome his fear of the unfamiliar, many preliminary visits were planned. His prospective parents first visited him at the institution, taking him for short walks and shopping trips, and then to their home to show him his room and possessions. When George was finally placed, his security was enhanced by simplifying his environment and providing him with consistent routines to con-solidate his trust in his new parents. Such routines included consist-ent, kindly discipline; clear, simple rules of behaviour; well-defined steps in eating, sleeping, dressing, and toileting; and limited social time with peers. These measures enabled the parents to keep George's world secure. As he and his parents adapted to each other, his deepen-ing trust gave him a base from which to move independently into new situations, asking questions, exploring, and anticipating answers. The consistent dependability of his life gave him reassurance. He took pride in achievement, and glowed with approval.

By age six, George was heavily reliant on his dependable family and seemed comfortably established with them. He was able to adjust to the arrival of an adopted younger sister with a combination of protec-tiveness and rivalry.

Through the years from age nine to 15, George's continuing fear of new events and challenges was evident in his perfectionist tendencies. He would attempt new ventures only if he were assured success. He progressed well through school, though he was always somewhat anx-ious about making mistakes. He entered into sports, but might bow out if he felt unsure of winning. He enjoyed contact with peers, but tended to boss and dominate. His healthy early immature dependence on his family had moved to the more mature level of dependent trust by the time he was 12 years old. He and his parents were in agreement about the pursuit of his goals.

By 15 years of age, George had learned to control his aggressive-ness with peers, and had close friends as well as an extended group of boy and girl acquaintances. His pleasant personality was an asset in selling advertising for his school magazine. He was highly effortful at school, and was meeting with academic success. His I.Q. took a remarkable leap in score. He enjoyed his adoptive family and his many relatives. His perfectionist tendencies were serving him well, as he had the capabilities and persistence to achieve his goals. By 18 years of age, George was enrolled in an out-of-town university.

At the time of his interview at age 30, George was an attractive, well-dressed, friendly, confident young man, and had a degree in psychology. He was financially comfortable as a salesman for a large company. He was happy with his job, though he stated that he still 'hates to fail or be criticized' and that he 'overcomes difficulties by trying harder.' His perfectionism found an outlet in his favourite hobby, woodworking, at which he excelled 'because [he had] the patience for it.' He had married a woman who shared his ideals; the pair were on good terms with both her family and his. George expressed warmth and protectiveness toward his family. He and his wife had friends whose company they enjoyed on weekends. During the week, they shared the housework in their home. George and his wife were flexible about their religious affiliations, attending either a Catholic or a Lutheran church. George regarded himself as a good money manager. He and his wife spent wisely (apart from the occasional 'blow-out'), and had acquired no debts other than a mortgage and car payments.

In retrospect, it is evident that George's early orientation as a 'watcher' permeated his lifelong development. His cautious approach to events was evident until he was 15 years of age. His reservations about tackling new challenges until he was sure of his ground, coupled with his perfectionist tendencies, indicated his need to feel safe and sure before committing himself to seek solutions. A further quality that distinguished George was his enthusiasm for carrying out a commitment once he decided to be involved. His early reluctance to trust his adoptive parents followed the same pattern that had been observed in the institution. However, once his trust was confirmed, he entered into family life and carried out his parents' expectations with total conviction. As he stated, 'One should put genuine effort into life.' Throughout his adolescence, George gained confidence both in his academic skills and in his worth as a human being. In adulthood, this confidence was expressed in his effective work habits, as well as in his trusting, comfortable relationships with his wife and both their families.

In the future, George will likely continue to function in a mentally healthy way.

Summary

The therapeutic approach selected for our institutionalized subjects was based on security theory and thus focused on the provision of consistent, loving care coupled with regular cognitive and social stimulation. Periodic evaluations based on developmental, rather than chronological, age allowed for broad variability in the children's developmental patterns. Temperamental variations also were observed to affect the manner in which individual children developed.

Adoptive placements were undertaken as each child was deemed sufficiently mature. Yet, even with careful judgment and preparation, many children exhibited regressive behaviours after settling in with their new family. Such regression might accompany any major transition in any child's life, and is not necessarily an indication of future problems in adulthood, as shown by the various case histories presented in this chapter.

4

Regression:
A Therapeutic Approach

The idea that regression could be an adaptive mechanism is inherent in security theory as well as in traditional psychoanalytic theory. This hypothesis was applied in rehabilitating the infants in the institution. It presupposed that all human children develop from birth to maturity in a series of predictable stages associated with chronological age. If a child is to achieve 'normal' development, each stage must be fully negotiated before proceeding to the next.[1] Furthermore, each individual has a unique pattern of development in social, cognitive, and motor skills.

A child who stalls in one or another area within a particular stage can be at a disadvantage in the next stage. Should nothing intervene to facilitate the stalled development, residual immaturities could create distortions and gaps in the following stage. The child might learn to compensate for these, but will never fully overcome them. Hence, cognitive tasks never fully mastered in infancy and the pre-school years can create learning problems in school. Similarly, disruption in the progressive attachment between parent and infant can create emotional and social deficits that may never be overcome. The infant's attachment to the mother, in particular, is the first and prototype of all later emotional and social relationships and thus provides the secure base from which all other development flows.

Rehabilitative Approach

At the inception of this study, the children in the institution ranged in age from a few weeks to three and one-half years. Although we were

1 Erikson, E. (1950). *Childhood and society.* New York: Norton.

aware of severe developmental deficits in the children even at five or six months of age, the focus of our study was on their mental health. Thus, we assumed that the distortions observed in the children's behaviour were due to emotional disturbance only. Hence, our expectation was that they would play when offered the opportunity; that they would welcome the opportunity to take control over such self-care as feeding and dressing; and that they would both accept and reach out for adult attention and affection.

Therefore, we provided them with the emotional support and activities that would be found in a healthy home. To our surprise, the children remained largely unresponsive and indifferent. It became apparent that monumental input would be needed to arouse these depressed children to any expectation that adult contact might be rewarding, and that opportunities for play and self-help might bring them satisfaction. As we sought ways to spark normal development, it became necessary to reduce adult expectations in order to accommodate the depressed level of function of these children. This practical approach soon became a strategy.

All our subjects had been deprived of that 'first' secure relationship (usually with the mother) from which subsequent trusting relationships flow. Hence, the first step in the rehabilitation of the children was to demonstrate the trust and interest that they should have experienced from the time of birth. Regardless of chronological age, each child was provided with a caretaker with whom to build this 'first' affectional relationship.

The adult provided care similar to that of a mother with her baby. The children were cuddled, patted, talked to, played with. The care was highly physical, tender, and protective. This intervention produced a gradual responsiveness on the part of the children and evidence of blossoming trust.

At the same time as we were working to arouse an affectional response toward caretakers, we exposed the children to a wide variety of play materials and play opportunities.

Observations

Surprisingly, the children remained unresponsive. The adults had not only to demonstrate how to play, but also to engage the children physically in the 'steps' of playing with toys. For example, an adult might repeatedly demonstrate a rattle, or might place a cylinder in a child's hands and manipulate it, arousing the child's interest and encouraging the child to experience movement. Very gradually, over many months, the children began to demonstrate age-appropriate play behaviour.

We believe that the principle of lowering the caretaker's expectations to meet the child's level of development helped to bring about behaviour that approximated age expectancy in both the affectional and self-initiated (effortful) aspects of the children's development. The older the children, the longer was the time required to reach these appropriate stages.

Despite the children's remarkable improvement within the institutional setting, it was not until they were placed in adoptive or foster homes that they demonstrated to what degree we had failed to provide a systematic series of experiences to 'normalize' both the affectional and the cognitive domains of their lives. Large gaps existed that would not have been observed in infants reared in homes where cumulative experiences would have been appropriately supplied through normal interaction with caretakers. The gaps in the children's cognitive experiences became even more evident as they entered school, where many of them demonstrated confusion and inability to pay attention to classroom activity.

Mark

Mark's case history exemplifies the importance of having emotional dependency needs met early in childhood. As we examine his history we sense a continuing unsatisfied need for immature emotional dependency. He had been in the institution for three years prior to the rehabilitation program. As his environment became more nurturing, his behaviour became increasingly 'normal,' and he was placed for adoption at four years, three months of age.

Although his response to the therapeutic program had been heartening, his personality structure remained fragile and his intellectual functioning uneven. After placement, his greatest need was to be allowed to regress, to be consistently cared for, to be loved and protected through new experiences until his infantile dependency needs were met. Only this would give him a secure base from which he could proceed toward normal development.

Mark's outgoing sociability, as well as his physical stature made him seem like an ordinary, active, alert four-year-old. His parents failed to grasp that his excitability in new situations indicated not eagerness and interest, but hyperactivity, and that his distractible behaviour was an expression of poor control. Furthermore, the behaviour patterns that were observed while he was in the institution became exaggerated when he was placed in his adoptive home. He continued to procrastinate and ask for help when dressing. He ate well, but dawdled. He resisted going to bed and had difficulty falling asleep. He played in an immature way with peers. His constant need for his mother's support was expressed by his following her everywhere and demanding attention, even when she discouraged this. Her insistence that he become more independent resulted in further clinging. She responded by nagging him. Mark's mother could not see that his exaggerated clinging signalled his unmet need for an immature reliance on his mother. When denied this fundamental security, Mark became anxious, as reflected in his poor sleep habits and eating behaviour.

Mark's case worker tried to convince his parents that his need for dependency was valid, given his history. She suggested they help him to wash and dress, and closely supervise his eating and playing. Mark needed to know that his parents' approval did not hinge on his demonstrating the competence of a 'normal' four-year-old. Despite this advice, Mark's parents continued to demand high achievement and exemplary behaviour from him; they could not accept this immature child. Their inability to allow him to regress made Mark increasingly high-strung and irritable.

A further complication was the adoption of a four-month-old brother when Mark was seven years old. This cuter, brighter, more manageable boy aroused feelings of guilt in the parents regarding their feelings toward their older son. Surprisingly, Mark displayed no overt jealousy toward the baby. Rather, he helped care for him, amused him, and shared treats and toys. This behaviour earned him approval from his parents and enhanced his status among his friends (this was *his* new brother!). A secondary reward was the baby's reaction to Mark: his brother's giggles made him glow with pride. Throughout his school years, Mark remained generally caring and solicitous toward his brother, even when his parents used the boy's exemplary behaviour to goad Mark. The two boys loved each other and depended on each other for companionship. Yet, their roles in the family became clearly defined: Mark was the rebellious underachiever, while the younger boy was the lovable, successful child.

The parent–child interactions during these years resembled an emotional see-saw. Mark's mother would make increasing demands that he grow up and show self-direction; Mark would temporarily cease to cling but would become withdrawn, angry, and frightened. His temper tantrums met with spanking. The social worker's intervention would create a lull in this continuing battle, but when relative stability was restored, the mother would increase her demands. The ensuing years witnessed Mark's losing battle for self-determination and his resultant loss of self-esteem. Under the guidance of the case worker, a variety of community supports were used to tide the family over crises: mental health clinics, reading clinics, psychological consultation. However, Mark and his family inevitably slipped back to their usual chaotic relationship.

Another complicating factor in Mark's development was a congenital heart murmur. Despite this, he appeared energetic and active until he was seven years old, by which time his heart rate was abnormally slow and his mother reported difficulty in rousing him from bed in the morning. Now labelled 'lazy,' Mark became tired and irritable, 'never finished anything,' and always had to be prodded. His sleep was disturbed. By the time he was 10 years of age, Mark had a serious heart problem, and by his late teens, doctors installed a pacemaker in his heart. He was now six feet, three inches tall. Although Mark's family were ambivalent toward him, they cared about him, and offered their support throughout his teens. They helped him through a minor brush with the law and, when he was 18, provided him with an apartment in their basement where he could live and entertain his friends.

Mark's school career was stormy despite his average intellectual potential. His size and early superficial sociability had encouraged his mother to enrol him in Grade 1, despite the social worker's warning that he was not ready, either socially or emotionally. This was the beginning of a pattern of recurring failure and repeated grades. His irate mother blamed the teachers and demanded that Mark do better, always rejecting recommendations for remedial classes for him. Fortunately for Mark, an assessment at age nine detected a confusion of right–left dominance. This condition persuaded his mother to accept special reading classes for Mark. The following year witnessed improved academic performance and general behaviour. But two years later – after he had been returned to mainstream classes – his problems resurfaced. By the time Mark was 14, his case worker convinced his mother that Mark would benefit from vocational school. With acceptable grades and his natural ability to work with his hands, Mark got a job working on machines at age 17. At last he seemed to have found something he enjoyed.

By the time our formal data collection was complete, Mark was 15 years old and still embroiled in conflict with his mother. His parents' acceptance of him was always qualified by their dissatisfaction with his performance as a son and as a student. His attitude toward his parents, in turn, was defensive. School and peer groups brought him little satisfaction. His brother was his only friend and source of support. Mark's future looked troubled.

When interviewed at age 30, Mark seemed a tired, ill man. Although his pacemaker was working imperfectly, he failed to keep doctor's appointments, smoked incessantly, and often missed meals. He had many debilitating physical symptoms, but pushed himself to keep working despite them. Since his early 20s he had had a variety of jobs as a machinist and as a tool maker. He liked his work and felt well paid, but he was still making payments on a truck and the house that he shared with his wife in a small city outside Toronto. Mark's skills made him feel productive and self-sufficient, but his chronic poor health sometimes left him feeling apathetic about his job and irritable with the people at work.

Although Mark had moved to another city to escape his over-controlling mother, he was still attached to her: 'I love my mother, but I hate her; she adopted children for all the wrong reasons.' His relationship with his father was warmer. He talked to his parents on the telephone every week or two or visited them about every second month. However, he would take no advice from either parent, nor could he accept any manifestation on their part of genuine concern or good will, 'because they can be very domineering, very condescending ... You feel like you are never going to grow up.' Mark's memory of a 'miserable childhood,' in which nothing he did was a success in the eyes of his mother, had precluded a healthy emancipation from his family. He remained hostile and defensive toward them, and as a result, insecure and vulnerable.

The only truly warm, accepting relationship that Mark had derived from his adoptive family was with his brother. Despite their differences in temperament and success, the two men still depended on each other and protected each other from parental criticism. Mark regarded his brother as his best friend. 'He has been very important to me, very supportive. He never criticizes me ... I think that was what took the edge off [the difficult times at home].'

At 30, Mark had few social skills and little interest in the companionship of peers; he was even phobic about crowds. Yet, he had married a friendly, comfortable woman who had a career as an electrolysis technician and followed her own interests. They shared home renovations, cooked and cleaned together, and went to the movies. They occasionally bickered over her shirking household responsibilities or Mark's leaving tools strewn over the house. On the other hand, Mark claimed that they 'laughed a lot,' and she said that he was a highly agreeable person to live with. Mark had a good relationship with his wife's family, though he saw them no more often than his own.

Mark and his wife appeared to have a cooperative and confident attitude toward the handling of their money. He felt that they had enough for their needs and could comfortably take care of their mortgage and truck. They planned no family until these debts were eliminated. They used credit cards for necessary purchases, and their money never ran out. He considered himself honest: 'I'm not going to cheat anybody, so I don't want to be cheated.'

Mark continued to find comfort in the religious faith of his childhood; perhaps it provided some safety in his chaotic life. He had attended separate schools with compulsory religious classes until he was nearly 16. He was an altar boy from age 11 until 15, and 'loved it,' possibly because church was predictable and reliable, unlike his home, which was in constant turmoil. Reflecting on life, he stated, 'God holds every card and if people will follow His rules He will look after them. When bad things happen to good people, it is merely a test of faith. If God interfered it would distort the Natural Laws. What will be, will be.' Mark's adult philosophy reflected an immaturely dependent blind faith and a belief in the 'logistics of life.' The Church had the answer to most problems, with the exception of overwhelming tragedy or death. He admitted to a recurring fear that he could not cope with tragedy on the basis of this logic, 'so I just forget about the possibility.' He was uncomfortable with the thought of loved ones dying. 'I hope I drop off first.' Table 3 evaluates Mark's security profile at age 30.

Summary

The social-theoretical notion that regression may be an adaptive mechanism in a child's development proved useful in rehabilitating our subjects within the institutional setting. Adjusting caretaker expectations to accommodate each child's level of development soon evolved from a practical strategy to become our therapeutic approach.

TABLE 3
Mark's security profile at age 30

	Independent Security (IS)	Mature Dependent Security (MDS)	Insecurity (I)	Immature Dependent Security (IDS)	Deputy Agents & Regression (DAR)
Family					
• parents			x		x
• siblings		x			
Social relations					
• partner		x			
• general			x		
Vocation	x				
Avocation	x				
Philosophy					
• money	x				
• religion				x	
• health			x		
Emotions			x		
Self		x			x

However, it was not always possible to maintain this approach once our subjects were placed in adoptive homes. When parents were unable to accept the behavioural and cognitive deficits in their adopted child, the home environment became a source of further stress for all, as in the case of Mark.

In retrospect, we learned from some of our initial placements the need to maintain and continue the strategy adopted in the institution once the children were placed in adoptive homes. Further, we began to recognize the difficulty facing our children in fathoming the complex and intense interactions that arise between family members: parent–child, parent–parent, parent–sibling, and sibling–sibling interactions presented a bewildering set of relationships for an adopted child to navigate.

For this reason, we soon learned to warn parents to expect immature and sometimes confused behaviour from our children, and provided them with specific guidelines to establish routines for eating, toileting, dressing, sleeping, and bathing. Close supervision of play with peers was recommended to avoid overstimulation, which could lead to a breakdown of social control. Such consistent daily patterns provided the safe, dependable world so essential to a child's feeling of security in the early stages of adoptive placement.

In general, those parents who were able to reduce their initial expectations and support their child through a period of immature behaviours experienced a smoother transition and a more comfortable adaptation within their family. This period of being 'babied' (ranging from several weeks to several months) allowed a child to consolidate a sense of acceptance and develop a feeling of belonging. Once this period was negotiated, most children seemed free to move toward more age-appropriate challenges.

5

The Need for Regression in Cognitive Function

The Rorschach Ink Blot Projective Test

In the initial phases of our study, the Rorschach Ink Blot Projective Test was used to assess the emotional state of the institutionalized children. Given as part of the regular battery of assessments at ages six, nine, 12, and 15 years, the Rorschach test also enabled us to track the course of the children's conceptual development as they made the transition from institution to homes, communities, and schools.

Since our subjects' concepts were shaped by their unusual early experiences, observations of their deviations from 'normal' development patterns proved useful. It was hypothesized that such knowledge might also have implications for children moving from one cultural or social milieu to another.

As our 28 subjects moved from the institution to their adoptive and foster homes, guidance procedures were initiated on the basis of clinical judgment. Meanwhile, analysis of the Rorschach data proved useful in two ways: (1) it confirmed the efficacy of some of the guidance practices that had been recommended to parents and teachers, and (2) it yielded insights into the children's behaviours as they passed through periods of regression.

Because it was impossible to analyse the data on all the children, records of 10 children representative of the group were selected for analysis (n = 10 children x four assessments each, or 40 records). Lacking a comparison group, we adopted the developmental norms elaborated by Ames, Metraux, and Walker.[1] The Rorschach was considered a particularly useful assessment for our subjects because of its unstruc-

1 Ames, L.B., Metraux, R.W., & Walker, R.N. (1971). *Adolescent Rorschach responses.* New York: Brunner/Mazel.

tured nature. It required the children to draw on their past experiences and their understanding of their environment to impose meaning on the blots, thus revealing their unique conception of their world. It was accepted that normal conceptual development could be characterized by stages reflected in the Rorschach responses, and that these would indicate a child's level of conceptual functioning.

According to Ames et al., a child's earliest response to the Rorschach test is typically global and diffuse. The percentage of whole (W) response is high, as is that for form (F). Form is perceived crudely and uncritically. As a child develops and is better able to discriminate differences, observed detail displaces some of these global responses. Emotional reactions appear and increasingly reflect structure and control. A dynamic integration between form and movement also appears. By six years of age, a child's conceptual development has reached a phase whereby he or she makes meaningful associations between ideas and recognizes the functional relationships underlying many aspects of experience. This integration is well established by nine years of age; as well, the child has become capable of considerable diversity and complexity of thought. This change is accompanied by improved mental acuity and quality of concept.

Improvement in acuity and quality is expected to continue until age 12, when evidence of even more complex and diverse thought patterns should be apparent. By age 15, there is a marked change when an adolescent is expected to experience temporary restriction of activity accompanied by withdrawal from authority figures. By now, the child is aware of personal problems and perceives some responsibility for their resolution. A child at this stage is often introspective, self-critical, and super-sensitive to emotional reactions. It is a transitory period of reflection on the path to maturity.

Observations

To what degree did the subjects in our study conform to the expected pattern of cognitive development? With the exception of one child, their development from age six years through age 12 showed a reversal of the 'normal' pattern. By six years, a home-reared child, having previously organized concepts around experiences since infancy, is ready to progress toward greater conceptual integration accompanied by keener understanding. By nine years, the integration is well established, and the child demonstrates greater flexibility and diversity of thought.

In contrast, our six-year-old institutional children, although demonstrating some confusion, showed considerable diversity of thought (more like that of a 'normal' nine-year-old), and seemed on the threshold of integrating concepts within normal expectation. However, by age nine, they seemed to have regressed to a more constricted level of function, although demonstrating greater keenness of understanding than that demonstrated at age six. By 12 years, they were once more within an expected range, moving toward diversity and flexibility of thought without sacrificing the quality and keenness of their responses. Unexpectedly, by age 15, little real change had appeared. Although reflecting healthy functioning, our children's profiles still resembled those of normal 12-year-olds. In terms of behavioural and intellectual control, there persisted a considerable reliance on external structures for solutions to problems, rather than a progression to solutions generated from their own thought processes.

An examination of the children's early experiences provided a rationale for such a pattern. In infancy, these children were both maternally and stimulus deprived. They were largely indifferent, even to their limited environment. Hence, there was little perceptual differentiation and little incentive to develop concepts. For example, they failed in their first year to grasp the notion of object permanence – i.e., that objects continue to exist even when they are out of sight. In their second year, many seemed not to differentiate between objects and people. As well, the lack of conversation among their early caretakers, coupled with the fact that the children were rarely spoken to, provided little encouragement to use their vocal apparatus. Even crying did not bring attention. Thus, their early experiences could not be organized by verbal labels, and vocalization was not perceived as a mode of communication. Thus, by three years of age, few children had verbalized more than one word – 'mama' – a generalized term for all caretakers.

After placement in homes, deficits in the children's concepts that had escaped detection in the institution emerged in the face of their expanded world. Firstly, the children were distractible compared with their home-reared peers. That is, they seemed to have difficulty in distinguishing central issues from irrelevancies: all stimuli pulled them, since they had so little early practice in organizing perceptions around a sound core of relevant information. Their impoverished early cognitive experiences precluded them from organizing and integrating their new family-based experiences in meaningful ways. They seemed either to force a new item of information into their inadequate, poorly organized conceptual framework, or to try to 'graft' it on, or to fail to understand it altogether. These children had difficulty recognizing functional relationships among ideas. They were slow to form mental links, which lack in turn inhibited their associating meaning with actions. For example, the statement 'Mother is going shopping' might be construed as 'Mother is leaving the house,' no appreciation of her mission. Concepts were also poorly grouped: for example, 'house' and 'family' might be associated, but 'parents' and 'siblings' might not. The children's limited fund of verbal concepts resulted in rigid thinking: a given word had only one meaning. This rigidity often precluded rethinking a statement in a flexible way. For example, if 'watch' signifies only a time-piece, then 'watch out' may have no meaning.

Sudden, unexpected fears also emerged. While dogs, cats, and birds were known to the children through stories, pictures, conversations, or in passing on the street, all had unanticipated characteristics when met in reality. The total sensory experience of 'knowing' an animal was very different from contemplating it in two-dimensional pictures. For example, living with a cat revealed the multitude of qualities not perceived before: the sensuous movement; the warm, deep fur; the intensity of its stare; its purr when content, or the emergent claws when thwarted; its characteristic postures, and so on. All these qualities, which home-reared children might easily organize into a conceptual framework, were lost to our subjects. Their preparation for family life had created many appropriate behavioural responses, but these often lacked depth and the enriched understanding that is born of day-to-day experience.

As another example, such simple concepts as 'clean clothes' or 'laundry,' although encountered in the institution, fell far short of a home-reared child's concept of the same objects or events. The institutionally reared children's understanding of 'laundry' and 'clean clothes' consisted of having soiled clothes taken off, placing them in a clothes hamper, and having them reappear at a later time, smelling clean and neatly folded in a drawer. In contrast, a child reared from infancy in a home where a parent does the laundry has a much more enriched sensory experience, as well as a cognitive awareness, of the process required to obtain 'clean clothes.' He or she experiences the fact that all the 'dirty clothes' are put together, removed to the basement or laundry room, and placed in a washing machine. Here the child smells the soap, sees the steam, hears the lid close, and hears the swishing of water. Later, the child may observe the parent take the clothes out and

place them in the dryer, from which they later emerge smelling fresh
and crackling with static. The child may particpate in the folding of
the laundry, or play under the ironing board. Then the parent takes
the clean clothes to various drawers and cupboards, from which they
later re-emerge for use. Such daily experiences are multiplied many
times in shopping, cooking, visiting friends, playing with siblings and
parents, having a pet, going on holidays, having a friend, and so on.

Similarly, as the children entered school, unexpected problems began to appear. Most of the children did not enter school until 6 years
of age, by which time both they and their parents were eager to em-
bark on this new phase of life. Before long, despite their initial enthusiasm, the children were restless, inattentive, and prone to irritate their
classmates. Parents and teachers were disappointed. Particularly, the
expectations of teachers were violated, as they had assumed that all
children in the class had backgrounds that were cognitively similar.
Their complaints led the case worker to intervene.

Interventions

In conjunction with the research team, a strategy of 'de-stimulation'
was employed: parents and teachers were counselled to reduce their
expectations and provide the children with structured, step-by-step
procedures that reduced the children's need to make choices. Simple
explanations and directives were recommended to reduce confusion.
De-stimulation appealed to teachers, as it not only reduced the pressure on the children, but on the teachers themselves.

Obviously, there had remained serious cognitive deficiencies in these
children's functioning that did not manifest within the limited structure of institutional life, but emerged as the children encountered the
complexities of life in homes, communities, and schools. We concluded
that our subjects had trouble selecting relevant from irrelevant stimuli
in their environment. Thus, de-stimulation consisted of 'stripping' routine events of extraneous people and objects, and providing only limited cues. Because the children's frustration threshold was low, the
presentation of too many materials, too complicated a pattern, or too
many choices precipitated loss of attention and emotional control. On
the other hand, simple tasks, simple explanations, and limited amounts
of materials presented one at a time were found to promote focus of
attention and reduce confusion. Further, parents and teachers were
urged to allow the children to remain in Grade 1 for more than one

year in an attempt to let their life experience catch up with those of their contemporaries.

The merit of this approach to overcome the cognitive deficits of early deprivation was confirmed by Rorschach data taken at age 15, as well as from the children's behaviour over time. By age 15, it was acknowledged that our subjects had achieved a level of function that, although immature, was within the normal stream of conceptual development, a considerable achievement in view of the severity of their early deprivation. Furthermore, their adaptation to home, school, and community appeared to be within normal expectations with no evidence of pathology. At that time, it was speculated that our subjects' Rorschach profile might reflect their response to the pressures of adolescence, which forced them to rely on simple structures supplied by external sources rather than internal (self-generated) structures. The question was raised whether this reliance on external systems for orientation and direction would be permanent. Lack of imagination and reflection, expressed as lack of sophistication in behaviour and lack of subtlety of thought, might always characterize this group.

One significant factor in the function of these children was the steady rise in intelligence quotient (I.Q.) from six to 15 years of age. Our particular group of 10 children showed a range in I.Q. from 96 to 124 by age 15, whereas at age six the average was 89. It was hypothesized that the nature of the intelligence tests, which are highly organized and require simple answers ('right' or 'wrong'), tapped the strengths of our subjects. Here, they did not need to employ imagination to score well. On the basis of the children's I.Q. scores, it is understandable that teachers and parents had higher expectations for achievement than these children were able to deliver. Our understanding of our children's behaviour was further enriched when the data were construed on the Vineland Social Maturity Scale, which revealed a social quotient of 12 years when our children's chronological age was 15. Such outcome was congruent with the children's conceptual functioning, whereby characteristics such as dependence on external structures and immature behavioural controls have common etiology.

Application beyond Research Study

Understanding our subjects' pattern of cognitive development has opened the door to a recognition of some of the difficulties faced by immigrant children (and their teachers) when school entry expectations are based on the assumptions and norms of the new culture. The same would apply to children reared in poverty. In terms of cognitive base, such children display many of the same inadequacies as our early-deprived subjects. In essence, they bring to the classroom an uneven and alien knowledge base, coupled with inadequate language skills in their adopted culture. Further, their early experiences have sometimes been chaotic and filled with uncertainty. The combination of cognitive inadequacy, social immaturity, poor nutrition, and emotional insecurity can create an overwhelming situation for both child and teacher. Clearly, the child needs time to grow into, and assimilate knowledge of, the new culture. The question is how to facilitate this process.

Some of the strategies adopted in this study might be directed toward culturally diverse communities. Schools could be a resource for both parents and children, as both must be engaged in the adaptive process. Drop-in facilities for parents and infants could be established to carry out such routines of daily life as eating, playing, and napping. The importance of consistency in building trusting relationships could be not only discussed but demonstrated in simplified daily procedures. Staff should include early childhood educators well versed in child development and able to relate to hesitant, troubled, and conflicted parents. Children of pre-school age, as well as those of school age unprepared for school entry, could benefit from preparation here, as could their parents.

Innovative training programs to allow older children to relive earlier normalizing experiences might prevent the confusion that often arises when overextended cognitive processes function on a frail base. In order to build consistent life experiences so that future events can be anticipated, daily routines should be instituted (breakfast, play time, nap, etc.). Such teaching would encourage mental links between past and future. Teaching modes should be developed to reinforce structure and direct thought and behaviour. Instructions and reasoning should be kept simple and logical. Play materials also should provide the opportunity to direct thought and behaviour. Activities that have a clear beginning, middle, and end would develop the concept of units of behaviour that had reasonable limits. Adult supervision would reinforce rules of social interaction (sharing, cooperation, emotional control). Limited stimulation in all aspects of living (rather than enrichment) should give time for understanding and internalizing some of the expectations of the adopted culture. Such a plan would place schools at the centre of the total education of families, and could re-place some of the variety of services that are currently offered piece-meal to immigrants. Present day care facilities within schools could be extended to include the participation of parents and older siblings as volunteers. While parents are taking language classes, infants and pre-school children could experience some of the customs, conventions, and foods of their adopted culture.

Innovative television programs and videos of cross-cultural family life could provide comparative models of child rearing, as well as the vocabulary to describe them and the opportunity for discussion. Home visits by social workers assigned consistently to the same families would provide the basis for trusting relationships and would reinforce the relationship between family, school, and community.

Summary

In order to monitor our subjects' cognitive function, data from the Rorschach Ink Blot Projective Test were gathered when the children were six, nine, 12, and 15 years of age. The patterns observed in their development differed significantly from those of home-reared chil-dren: at six years of age, our subjects displayed greater diversity of thought, but by age nine their cognitive level was more constricted. By age 12 conceptual function had normalized, but by age 15 subjects had not progressed beyond a normal 12-year-old's level of social and emo-tional maturity.

The children's need for regression was supported, at home and in the classroom, by interventions geared to 'de-stimulate' their environ-ment, such as creating simple, structured routines for daily activities. Some children were encouraged to repeat a school grade to enable them to attain a level of maturity comparable to that of their peers.

Future research might profitably explore how similar interventions might be applied to children moving from one cultural or social milieu to another.

6

Consistency:
The Road to Trust

Role of the Case Worker

A unique aspect of this study was the dedication of the case worker who participated from its inception (1956) to its termination 30 years later. Her constant presence and willingness to be called upon at any time by parents and children established a foundation of trust that was undoubtedly a factor in the surprisingly good level of mental health attained by the children at ages 15 through 18 years. Although the second phase of the study officially terminated and funding ceased at this time, some parents and children continued to contact her intermittently thereafter to share highlights of their lives. This interest continued even up to and beyond the termination of phase III. What particular magic created such a warm and enduring relationship, given the less-than-ideal conditions of a long-term university and social-agency based research project?

The personal qualities of the case worker undoubtedly helped this project to succeed. Her intelligence, her warmth and good humour, and her boundless physical stamina were enhanced by her background in obstetrical nursing, her short-term courses in social work, and her two years' postgraduate study at the Institute of Child Study of the University of Toronto. This knowledge of child development and parent education equipped her to identify the needs of children from infancy to maturity. She developed a sensitivity that permitted her to 'put herself in the shoes' of a growing child.

This case worker's knowledge allowed her to set goals for therapeutic interventions across two dimensions: (1) for the group, when the children were in the institution during phase I of the study, and (2) for individuals, after they were placed in adequate homes. Her knowledge also enabled her to estimate the degree to which the children were delayed or distorted in their development and to find ways of charting their progress.

The case worker knew that wide individual differences exist within any group of children, and she recognized that these were exaggerated to an extreme with our subjects. Her research training at the Institute of Child Study had emphasized the importance of accurate record keeping and motivated her to record daily, weekly, and monthly reports on the activities of the children within the institution and after their placement in homes. In addition to collecting the planned research data, all information from parents and schools – every contact, even by telephone – was recorded. Such detail provided an accurate source for child management strategies as well as for our research project.

The concepts of security theory (as described in Chapter 2) provided a central focus around which child management strategies could be organized. The case worker was not only familiar with these concepts but was adept at translating them into lay terminology. As security theory was applied developmentally, it provided the guidelines for therapeutic interventions within the institution when the children were infants and pre-schoolers. Once the children were in their adoptive homes, and again at school entrance, security theory provided a frame of reference as the shift in the balance from dependence to independence took place between parent and child. The theory was constantly re-interpreted as the children approached early adolescence. The case worker made herself available at all times, providing guidelines for parents to follow as they worked toward achieving security – and thus mental health – for their children. Furthermore, the case worker never limited herself to counselling our subjects only. Rather, the whole family – siblings, fathers, mothers, grandparents – received advice if it were sought, and sometimes even if it were unsolicited. Such genuine caring and steady attention to the needs of each family created a great bulwark of trust.

The case worker's role in the study assumed two dimensions that were fashioned around the concept of security: (1) her relationship to the children's families and the degree to which they needed support as a unit, (2) the children under study and the degree to which their mental health could be fostered by their parents. Thus, the case worker was an advocate for the child within the family and the community, and was also able to assess families along a continuum of security.

Some families, unsure of their parenting skills, assumed an *imma-ture dependent relationship* with the case worker, relying on her to supplement their lack of knowledge about child development and leaning on her for specific directives about their child's appropriate routines, play times, play with neighbourhood children, discipline, school, and even manners. As such strategies succeeded and parents gained more skill and confidence, their relationship with the case worker became more reciprocal, with parents and worker sharing information and discussing together what might be the most appropriate strategies for their child. The nature of this relationship was that of *mature dependent trust.*

Other families quickly formed a relationship with the case worker that was largely dependent on her guidance yet was based on their own successful past experience with children and their good sense in dealing with the child placed with them. These were the *independently secure* people who acted as true collaborators on the research project. Still other families formed a relationship with the worker that was based on their reliance on *deputy agents.* Such families, although not always willing to rely on the case worker's guidance, nevertheless clung to her visits and maintained intense contact with her over the years. They may have viewed the worker as a status symbol in the context of a university research project, or as a safety net when problems seemed insurmountable. Such relationships were often characterized by fran-tic demands for immediate attention when an emergency arose and, at the same time, an inability to continue to accept the worker's recom-mendations once the crisis was past.

The central premise of the case worker's guidance was that trust in others, in oneself, and in one's world is the core of mental health. An attitude of trust is attained in early infancy as the result of predictable and dependable care. A child who grows in trust begins to impose order and meaning on experience and eventually recognizes his or her relationship to the trustworthy people in the world. Through their re-lationship with consistent caretakers, children develop feelings of self-worth. As they become progressively more confident, they can extend those good feelings to others and invite new experiences. Thus the two requirements for good mental health in early childhood are: (1) dependable, consistent adults who can be relied on for care and encouragement, and (2) opportunity for independent action that leads to the development of self-confidence.

Hence, after a child was placed in the adoptive home, the first sign of mental health that the case worker looked for was immature dependency. This would be revealed by the child's comfortable acceptance of parental care. A later sign was independent security, displayed by a child's grasping opportunity for independent action. A still later sign, that of mature dependent security, was the child's successful interaction with contemporaries. A warning sign was any indication that the child was dealing with insecure feelings in potentially unhealthy ways. These might include reliance on deputy agents or defence mechanisms such as undue crying, excuses, lying, rationalization, 'sour grapes,' stealing, etc. All these signs and symptoms could be used as a basis for planning parental strategies.

It was the case worker's difficult role to apply these concepts of security theory to each of the 28 children in the study, individually. This implied (1) a recognition of the developmental level of function of each child as reflected in his or her behaviour, and (2) an assessment of the depth of dependent trust already established in the child's personality prior to placement. Having once assessed this, through familiarity with a child's personality and past experiences, the case worker's next challenge was to interpret this information to adopting or foster parents. Such interpretation was tempered by the parents' expectations for their child and their capacity to identify the ways and means of building dependent trust in a child of vulnerable mental health.

One of the barriers to understanding between parent and child was the parents' lack of awareness that these children were coming to their families with a very frail self-concept. Unlike most pre-school children, who have almost unwittingly integrated their parents' values through thousands of experiences from birth, these children came as strangers, not only to their family, but also to the expectations of their culture. Had their lives been normal, they would have been exposed to developmentally appropriate caretaking as they grew through the relative helplessness of early infancy. Thus, increasingly complex experiences would have been provided them according to their capacity to understand and integrate these into a consistent cognitive structure. Without this sensitive early caretaking, the children brought to their families sparse value systems that their new parents might neither appreciate nor approve. Furthermore, could the children have had normal infant experiences with their families, the mere presence of parents would have ensured a consistency in expectations of what chlidren ought to do and not do. In this way, values would have been transmitted subtly and largely without conflict. Yet, such a process was clearly impossible once the children had passed infancy. The question was – how to insure the transmission of family values as quickly as possible?

As children learn most rapidly in a consistent environment that allows them to predict the outcomes of their actions, it was expedient for the case worker to help the parents achieve consistent parenting strategies within the family unit. For this reason, she frequently wrote down timetables for children's daily, weekly, and even monthly activity, and reassessed these constantly. Many telephone calls and interviews were required. Discipline strategies were worked out that de-emphasized punishment and concentrated on learning from mistakes. The case worker trod a fine line between the expectations of the parents and the limitations of the children.

The case worker and the research team shared the belief that the degree of success of each child's placement depended on the relationship that could be consolidated with the family. Thus, much effort was directed toward establishing mutual trust. Most families received their adopted or foster child with a full heart, ready to accommodate their child as best they could. However, this willingness was circumscribed by the family constellation and their preconceived notions of how children should behave. Therefore, the first task of the case worker in building a relationship was to acknowledge the parents' feelings and good will while realistically evaluating the degree to which each member of the family could adapt to the demands of a new child. In assessing a family's strengths and vulnerabilities, she took into consideration: the personalities, ages, and school achievement of the siblings; the parenting capabilities of the new mother; the degree to which the father supported his wife's efforts and opinions; and to what degree the extended family offered support. The aspirations of each family for their natural children in school and community were considered important, because the adopted child also would likely be expected to live up to them. The religious beliefs of a family were also moderating factors.

Within this context, the case worker attempted to interpret the needs of the new child and present a realistic definition of his or her capabilities and limitations. A crucial factor in her success was the accuracy with which she could assess how much information a family could make use of at one time, and what information she should withhold for future contacts. Finally, she recognized that trust would build as a result of her ready availability whenever parents needed help.

The other side of this sensitive relationship was the degree to which she understood these children who were being placed. Her familiarity with these children, from her personal contact with them within the institution as well as her consistent longitudinal records, allowed her a realistic evaluation of each child's strengths and vulnerabilities and the degree to which each had overcome the effects of early deprivation. She could spell out in behavioural terms where developmental, affectional, and social delays could be seen (e.g., 'a four-year-old can usually play with other children quite happily for an hour, but Evan still needs to be limited to half an hour, before he becomes disruptive'). Her knowledge of each child's limitations enabled her to advise parents on comfortable daily routines that would prevent the child's behaviour from disintegrating through lack of emotional control and uncertainty over parental expectations (e.g., 'Evan, age four, should have a clearly defined daily schedule'). A typical routine might be:

7:00	Awake and up
7:30	Breakfast, wash, dress, play time alone, help with chores, etc.
9:30	Outside – play with peers, 1/2 hour to 3/4 hour
10:15	Snack time with mother and siblings; reading, television, etc.
11:45	Lunch
12:30	Sleep or rest (quiet time)
1:30	Play time – out with parents, etc.

Such a routine would be evaluated weekly and modified according to the child's response to it. A happy, relatively self-controlled child was a signal that he or she might be ready for more extensive and prolonged activities.

The case worker was able to forewarn parents that the children's lack of experience in their new lifestyle, as well as their lack of sophistication in the use of language, could lead to misunderstandings. Therefore, parents were advised to use relatively short directives that were clearly defined. Furthermore, steady progress should not be expected in the children's adaptation to home, school, and community life. Periods of regression should be respected, as these would allow the children time to consolidate small gains and give them confidence to participate in new experiences. In addition, parents were alerted to the fact that transitions in the children's experience – such as holidays, family visits, going to school, joining scouts, going to camp, and participation in confirmation – could be expected to create confusion and anxiety, and therefore should be carefully planned.

The case worker herself often supported both parent and child by accompanying them to hospitals, testing sessions, school interviews, psychiatrist's appointments, and so forth. As a way of giving total support to families, she might offer to babysit for an overstressed mother, or intervene in anticipation of a problem that had escaped the unsuspecting eye of a busy parent. She would arrange for assessments for siblings when their problems threatened to upset the balance of the whole family. As the children grew into early adolescence, she would sometimes treat them individually to lunch or a special show.

Thus, her role as advocate for each of our subjects was broadly defined. Her support and intervention reflected her recognition that the health of the children would falter should the family unit become disrupted. The effectiveness of this style of advocacy was evaluated in a questionnaire to parents as phase II of the study approached its end. (This questionnaire, along with parents' responses, appears in Appendix 2.) All the families responded. The theme that ran through each response was that this case worker was a longterm, readily available friend of the family whose intervention built confidence and trust.

To illustrate the way the case worker related to families within the context of security theory, we can examine her relationship with Kevin and his parents.

Kevin

Kevin's strengths and weaknesses were well known to the case worker at the time of his adoptive placement. While in the institution, he had shown a capacity for strong attachments to caretakers. This ability to relate helped him endure many new situations, which created undue fears in him. He seemed unusually apprehensive about new experiences (which trait may have reflected his high intelligence), and needed much adult support to overcome his initial resistance. However, once he allowed himself to participate in a new event, he would be flooded with the pleasure of it and would sweep people along with him as they shared his joy. Increasingly, he demonstrated the two critical assets for a mentally healthy child: (1) a capacity for dependent relationships, and (2) enjoyment of effort. These qualities were decided assets when we were planning Kevin's placement with a family.

Although the case worker anticipated Kevin's apprehension about this new situation, she counted on his ability to put his trust in adults to carry him through. His new family were encouraged to give him warmth and understanding. Recognizing Kevin's need to regress, the case worker made specific recommendations for the steps needed for him to put down roots and form an immature dependency on his parents. This was to be done through establishing consistent routines for his eating, sleeping, dressing, and toileting. Rules regarding play and social activities were to be enforced in a kind and affectionate way.

His parents were forewarned that Kevin's undue fears would likely inhibit displays of normal, effortful behaviour. Further, the case worker advised them on how they might support him through stressful situations, e.g., carry him, hold him, forewarn him. Hence, the worker's aim, within the context of security theory, was to allow this four-year-old boy to regress – to become immaturely dependent on his parents and to experience the satisfactions of moving gradually toward independent effort.

This family initially leaned on the case worker in an immaturely dependent way. Yet, they made good use of her knowledge and advice while they slowly gained confidence in their own capabilities to devise and evaluate parenting strategies. Finally, they moved to independent status with the worker, maintaining a steadfast friendship with her.

Kevin's adjustment to his adoptive family, and theirs to him, was congenial, on the whole. Kevin showed consistent and rewarding development in the intellectual, emotional, and social aspects of his life. At 18 years of age he was a relatively self-confident boy with deep roots in his family, satisfactory friendships, and plans to attend university. His adult profile at age 30 was one of commendable mental health.

Suzanne

Suzanne's story illustrates how the case worker adapted to the unique circumstances of each child.

Suzanne, a child with an Ojibwa heritage, was placed from the institution into a white, middle-class suburban family when she was two years of age. This rather rigid family expected high achievement from their own five children and aspired to a high standard of living (big house, several cars). Suzanne made a satisfactory adjustment to this family, as they did to her. They accepted her immaturities and relatively slow rate of development. Suzanne's three main developmental problems, which recurred throughout her life, centred around (1) her somewhat fearful relationship with her strict foster mother, (2) her struggle to be legally adopted into her foster family, and (3) the reconciliation of her native heritage. Over time, her passive nature led to a poor relationship with her foster mother; she related more comfortably to her foster father and siblings. Not until she was 11 years of age did she seem a fully integrated member of the family. By this time she was expressing a strong desire to be adopted by them, rather than just fostered. Despite this desire, foster care was continued because her family perceived a necessity to recover expenses for her care from the agency. Adoption was not to be completed until she was nearly 18 years of age.

While pressing her family to adopt her Suzanne was also reconciling her conflict over her native origins. Her case worker was able to help her with this in various ways. A visit to an Indian reserve was arranged, followed by discussion with some of its residents. Books on native culture and the history of the Ojibwa tribes revealed some of the strengths of her background. This interest led Suzanne to collect native poems, many with contemporary themes. These she put into a book, which she presented to her worker.

Although Suzanne had limited verbal skills, she developed a talent for writing. Her feelings poured from the letters she wrote to her case worker from time to time. In these, one finds a progressive zest for life as she passed through rebellious feelings against her mother, unhappy feelings about North American prejudice against Indians, and resentment about parental supervision. Her letters seemed to provide a safety valve for the resolution of resurgent, uncomfortable feelings. The following excerpts from her letters reveal some aspects of her development from adolescence to young adulthood.

(Age 14 years, 11 months)

Dear Miss K—,

Hi, I love my bike! I rode it one Saturday and I couldn't stop riding! I nearly got myself lost! I rode all over the place. I usually ride with my girlfriend, Nancy. Remember her? We're going skating on Thurs I think. Then swimming on Friday for sure and my two girlfriends, they're both Indians, one's straight from India. They might come. My girlfriend, Joti, she's Indian and she's dark, and I was wondering why I wasn't that dark. My other girlfriend, Manisha, she is so fun to hang around with. She is a Hindu Indian.

Nancy had to stay one night for English, and her teacher said I could wait for her and so I did, and her teacher asked me what nationality I was and I said Canadian Indian, Ojibwa, and she asked me what tribe I was from, Six Nations or around Lake Huron? and I said I don't know and I wanted to tell her so much to and I didn't know! Unless I forgot. I felt so stupid when I said I didn't know. I want to know.

You know that dog I never stop talking about, Kelly? Well one night she was hit by a car, and they had to put her away. The day I heard about it, I cried so much because I loved her very much and now she's gone and I'll never see her again. I was so close to her and she could hardly wait till I got out of the door before she jumped all over me and that little tail of her's nearly wagged right off. I always had a bone for her or a piece of meat. During the winter when she came to see me she would shiver and I would lock her up and wrap her up in my coat. During the summer I would take her swimming every night. She would run back and forth and bark at me and sometimes fall right in. Then we would be on our way back and my dad would be sitting there ready to go for a walk with her. She loved my dad and my dad really was fond of her. She would protect me from the paper boy every day. She would make us laugh when she would get excited and run all over the place barking. Now she gone.

Thank you for the letter and the picture. I really like it and I will keep it forever. My mom is really proud of me and same with my dad. The neighbours are pretty surprised about it. Thank you Miss K.

Love,

Suzanne

(Age 16 years, eight months)

Dear Aunt M—,

Hi, How's everything with you? I mean it, I just don't know what the hell's wrong with me. I feel like dying. so what else is new?

I don't know why, but I told my parents Peter's 10-speed bike was stolen from the garage and it wasn't! I lost it up at the plaza. I lied to them. I did tell them the truth and they're mad at me, which I don't blame them. I have to pay Peter $60.00 for my punishment is that I can't buy my own 10-speed that I've wanted so bad. You don't know how much I wanted that bike, I sold my old bike for $30.00 and I was going to help pay for my new 10-speed, now I can't even buy one. It was probably Mother's idea of a punishment and my dad announced it, because he never knew I wanted that bike. I hate her so much, she makes me so miserable. She's not my mother, my mother's DEAD. She constantly checking up on me. Last weekend, a friend of mine, John called me, and I asked to go to Michele's like an idiot, and she says 'what, are you going to meet John there?' God, she's gets me mad.

I think I'd be happier an orphan, I don't care if I would be poor or what, as long as I was happy, I don't know, but I think she's got something against me. What's the age adopted people can leave there home legally. Please tell me.

One of the patients at the Bayview Villa [where Suzanne volunteered] called me a dirty Indian Bitch. Friendly aren't they? For no reason. She had asked one of the tea girls for cereal for dinner, so I told the tea girl and she said to the old lady that it wasn't allowed. She told her friends I was a Dirty Indian Bitch.

Oh well, I don't care. I think I'll go for a long walk, try to settle down. so please think about it ok. I do hope you can come, if you can't there will be other times.

Love,

Suzanne

(Age 17 years, two months)

Dear Aunt M—,

Hi, I miss my favourite aunt you know! When you don't phone, or write, I write to you and tell you how I'm doing! Well, I'm just doing GREAT!!! I'm just bubbling over with happiness. Believe me, I couldn't be happier!!

The fighting with my mom is ALL FINISHED!! I could actually feel myself grow out of that 'age period'! I'm not fooling! All of a sudden, I wanted to talk to my mom, I wanted to go places with her, I wanted her around, I wanted to be around her! It was so amazing! Every day after school, I come home, I have coffee with her, we talk.

...

School is going great! I got my report, and I failed my typing, 41! So this term, wow, I gotta get at least a 59! I pray to the Lord I get 59!

Last semester, I failed Graphic Arts, the final report, a fail, so I went to the guidance counsellor, and he straightened me all out, and now, New Year, I only take four courses, and I get my grade 12 diploma, then I can go on to where ever I want to, so I think I'll go onto Seneca College.

So I gotta work like a fool idiot this term! I can't fail my typing. I just can't!

...

I'm doing embroidery right now, on material. I read this beautiful poem, and I wanted it on material, so away I went, and I'm almost finished. The poem goes like this:

If you Love something;
Set if Free,
If it Returns,
It is Yours;
If it doesn't
It never was.

Isn't that beautiful? So I've got a white bird flying in the sky, and then the poem underneath it, and below the poem, I've got a black horse walking through tall grass, and along the sides I'm going to put in some flowers. I hope it turns out, cause if it does, I'll do more!

Oh, Aunt Mary, You don't know how HAPPY I am! I just feel like running across a field screaming at the top of my lungs.

...

Come and visit sometime! I can't wait to see you!

Love,

Suzanne

(Age 21 years, eight months)

Dear Aunt M—:

hi, thanks so much for the beautiful Indian note paper. It's really beautiful. They're all so cute, I'd like to frame a few.

Its been so long since I've written to you and I have so much to tell you. I haven't seen you since September.

How was your Christmas and New Year's? Mine was really great. We had the whole family together, 2 new members, Geoff and Doreen had a baby boy, his name is John after my dad. Is he ever cute! He is just the happiest little guy. The sweetest little smile in the world. I just love him so much I was constantly picking him up and playing with him. He loves Katey. Katey is 3 ½ now, almost 4, her birthday is in June, John will be 2 in July. I can't wait, because when Katey turned 1, I made her a rug with her name on it, so I'm going to do the same with John. At the end of September, I lost my job at Montreal Trust. My manager said she didn't think I was suitable for the job. I think it was my leg, all the time I had off, and they needed someone full time.

...

Last week I met my [natural] brother. Is he ever nice. He's just like Al, so friendly and always laughing. he is 31. He lives in North Bay with his Indian wife 'Jo' from Six Nations Reserve.

They have two boys, and a new born baby girl. She called it Michelle Nicole. My sister Sandy is supposed to be having her baby anytime now. Bonnie and Marlene and Sandy live in Collingwood.

I also met my [natural] sister Nada. She lives in Toronto. She's 21. She lives at The Indian Girl's residence on Spadina. She is *really* mixed up – confused. I really don't know the whole story but the whole family is rejecting her. I think that is *stupid!* She tried to kill herself once and to me that is a cry for help and there's is no one to help her. I don't care what the others say I like her and I want her to know I'm there if she needs someone. Bonny also likes her. Bonny likes everyone and everything. She's so sweet and sincere. I really love Bonny. She's such a lovable person and she's my sister!! Wait till you meet her, you'll love her. I have so many pictures of all my nieces and nephews! They're all so cute, big brown Indian eyes.

Well, I guess I better go now. I'll write more *often* I promise. Bye, Aunt M—, and thanks again for the beautiful gift.

Love,

Suzanne

When interviewed at age 27, Suzanne once more appeared to be the passive, subdued person that characterized her social manner through-out her early life. Her difficulty in verbalizing her feelings, and the shortness of her responses to the interviewer (her former case worker), gave the impression of a rather flat, uncreative, and unresponsive young woman. There was no evidence of the high-spirited, sensitive, emotional girl who had written those soaring letters during her growing years.

Suzanne had emancipated herself from her family amicably. At age 22, she left a well-loved live-in boyfriend and drove to Alberta with one of her sisters. There she remained, working in a variety of well-paid jobs in a frontier town. She seemed pleased with her life despite its relative isolation, and was delighted to be living according to her own rules. She was saving money to return East eventually. She returned home to comfort her father on her mother's death when she was 27 years old.

Two years later, Suzanne was home once more, ill herself and needing care. Her father and adopted siblings rallied around her, giving comfort and nursing until she was hospitalized, at which time they called the case worker to inform her of Suzanne's serious illness. Shortly after the worker's visit at the hospital, Suzanne died of cancer. Her case worker attended the funeral.

Summary

Security theory holds that an individual seldom maintains a static emotional state but rather is constantly in pursuit of feelings of personal security or serenity. Such a belief parallels the Piagetian notion that an individual is always actively involved in seeking out, acting upon, and maintaining equilibrium in the environment. In so doing, one increases the likelihood of optimal adaptation.

Our team's work with families and their children reflected the conviction that healthy adaptation was always possible. The research team was a crucial source of support to the case worker for consultation and evaluation of her ongoing practice. As for case worker, her role was manifold. She acted as an objective observer to anticipate obstacles and forewarn parents to modify their child's environment. She acted as a catalyst to help create conditions that would encourage the child's best effort. Finally, she provided steady, non-judgmental support to further the well-being of each family.

Such enduring and close relationships with families demanded a wealth of emotional stamina and sound judgment. Times of self-doubt and discouragement were inevitable. The fact that the research team and the case worker shared a consistent philosophy and met frequently for discussion, questioning, and reaffirmation was undoubtedly a contributing factor to the success of the case worker's mandate. Further, the availability of test data, which could be used for guiding families, teachers, and school principals, provided reassurance for her decisions.

7

Finding Their Way: Adaptation

Intellectual Assessment of Our Subjects

Our initial interest in examining the intellectual functioning of the children in our study was to determine to what degree they might overcome their early intellectual deficits. Of further interest was the length of time such recovery might take.

To assist in setting up the rehabilitative program, the Bayley Infant Developmental Assessment was employed in the hope of gaining some insight into the level of each child's development and a profile of the child's pattern of functioning. Unfortunately, the depressed state of the children precluded their relating to the tester, the materials, or the criteria of the early developmental tests. It was not until the children had been exposed to the rehabilitation program for more than a year that any realistic estimate of their level of function was possible. Therefore, a formal program of assessment was delayed until each child reached six years of age. At age six, each child was tested on the Binet Intelligence Scale, and again at ages nine and 12. The Wechsler Intelligence Scale for Children (WISC) was used at fifteen years of age.

By the time the children were 15 years of age, when the final analysis was done, it was apparent that, as a group, they had overcome their early impairment. In fact, remarkable recovery had taken place by six years of age, as reflected by the fact that no difference of statistical significance was evident on full scores of the group between six and 15 years of age. However, examination both of group patterns of functioning and of individual profiles revealed more meaningful information.

From ages six to 15, a few children never rose beyond their early low score, while other children showed dramatic increases. As well, most of the children performed consistently higher on performance tests than on verbal items. By 15 years of age, 19 of 23 subjects were superior in performance tasks. Yet, the deficiency in verbal scores was not indicative of severe impairment. Unexpectedly, our group as a whole demonstrated competence in similarities and Block Design WISC items (this, even above age expectancy), an accepted measure of abstract logical thinking.

Such a pattern led us to hypothesize that most of our subjects were in the process of developing mental capabilities that might serve them satisfactorily as they adapted to social expectations. However, as yet, they had been unable to develop a correspondingly rich and flexible vocabulary to describe objects and events. Our hypothesis was bolstered by the group's performance in school, where most of them were proceeding according to age expectancy, but without displays of academic excellence.

As our study progressed, our interest in the information from the intellectual assessments broadened. Although we were aware that intellectual scores were related to school achievement, the question arose whether these might also be related to later success at work. A reasonable assumption was made that the skills and attitudes that foster school achievement might also be a component of later work habits. Further, the question was raised that a higher intelligence quotient (I.Q.) might correlate with a subject's having a wider range of life choices than a subject with a lower I.Q. Such an advantage might provide greater potential for successful adaptation.

When the adult interviews were carried out in phase III, our interest was in the overall adaptation to life's demands. It was assumed that an individual's level of adaptation would reflect a combination of constitutional endowment, value system, sense of security, intellectual competence, motivation, and persistence. The balance of these factors would provide some explanation for our subjects' behaviours. Would it be possible to isolate to what degree I.Q. at age 15 might predict adult adaptation?

It was assumed that success in work requiring extensive knowledge and organizational skills would reflect a higher I.Q. than success in work that required only narrowly defined skills. It was expected that successful work performance in adulthood would be adequately compensated financially, enabling our subjects to be self-supporting.

When our adult data on work performance and self-support were summarized, we discovered one group of eight subjects whose I.Q.s had ranged from 105 to 128 at 15 years of age. Of this group, four had obtained university degrees and were employed in positions requiring managerial and organizational skills. Each was performing satisfactorily. Their I.Q.s at age 15 had been 128, 119, 115, and 109, respectively. Three others of this eight were successfully self-employed. Their I.Q.s at age 15 had been 112, 124, and 105, respectively. One other subject whose I.Q. was 110 at age fifteen was self-employed and performing adequately.

A second group of six subjects whose I.Q.s at age 15 had been 80, 83, 84, 86, 93, and 96, respectively were performing remarkably capably and had stable work histories. All were self-supporting, and in some instances, were supporting families. They were employed in such positions as sous-chef in a private club, manager of a supply centre for a large company, and nursing assistant.

Applying our criteria, we concluded that for seven of the first group of eight, accurate prediction of later function on the basis of I.Q. could have been made. On the other hand, for all six subjects in our second group, predictions would have underestimated their later competent level of function.

Among the rest of our subjects, only two demonstrated unstable work habits and erratic lifestyles. These young women had demonstrated frail personalities from infancy, and as adults seemed to lack a clear sense of self, showed little capacity to sustain relationships with partners, and found parenthood difficult. These subjects had I.Q.s of 76 and 93, respectively, at 15 years of age.

Considering our subjects as a group, our assumption that later work competency might be predicted from I.Q. and school performance had to be relinquished. Obviously, other characteristics accounted for later competence.

Examination of individual histories indicated powerful elements in our subjects' personalities that revealed clues to their successful life adaptation. Each individual had a unique combination of strengths and weaknesses. We isolated a few characteristics that seemed to give strength to later function. One was a persistence in pursuit of goals; a second was a capacity to relate comfortably to adults and peers; a third was the belief in some religious or philosophical system; and a fourth was a controlled level of anxiety in pursuit of goals.

Following is a remarkable example of a highly functioning young man at age 32.

David

David's performance on the Binet scale never rose above 72, and his final WISC at age 15 showed a pattern of 83 (full score), 72 (verbal score), and 97 (performance score). By age 32 he was married, owned a home, two cars and a cottage, supported his wife and two children, and had held one responsible job for eight years as a manager of supplies for a drug store chain. Later, he had been employed as a highly skilled technician in an electrical supply company. His history reveals early characteristics that evidently took precedence over measured intelligence in shaping the boy and the man he was to become.

David lived the first six years of his life in the institution and was four years old when the rehabilitation program started. At this time, he displayed anxiety and lack of trust in his new environment. Compulsive behaviour, such as thumb sucking and constant flushing of toilets, emerged. By the time he was five years old, he began to relate to new adults, but had yet to form a single trusting relationship. He was now interested in toys and books, and was noisy and sociable. Increasingly, he showed a desire for a neat and tidy little world that he could control as expressed in such behaviour as folding his clothes. When faced with difficult tasks, David's frustration exploded into temper tantrums.

When he was six years of age, David was placed with his volunteer 'aunt' as a foster child. Here he was babied, rocked, kissed, and treated like the child he was emotionally and intellectually, rather than as would be expected for his chronological age. He was thrilled with his new life and foster parents: 'How lucky I am!' 'Do I have to go back?' 'Auntie, will you rock me a little?' Visits to the family cottage and contact with relatives there were a delight. A relaxed atmosphere in this setting, and kindly firm rules for discipline, provided David with a secure world, which in turn increased his confidence and assertiveness. His foster father took an active role in David's life, for example, taking him to the park to play ball. By age seven, David was verbalizing his identification with his family: 'I don't ever say I don't want to go to bed, because Auntie is too nice. She is the best girl I ever had.' He was increasingly sensitive to his foster mother's health and feelings. His request to call his foster parents 'Mother' and 'Father' was refused, and so he continued to address them as 'Auntie' and 'Uncle.'

When David was seven and one-half years old – 18 months after placement – his foster father died. David was surprisingly solicitous and protective toward his foster mother, although clinging to her at the same time: 'I guess I will have to be the daddy.' He was conscientious about his chores, ran errands, comforted her: 'Crying won't get you anywhere, Auntie.' 'Sit down and relax.' 'Isn't it nice to have a little boy like me, Auntie?' 'Could I sit on your knee for a little while?'

Relatives rallied to help David and his mother. He was invited on trips, taken to games, included in cottage life until he felt he belonged. By eight years of age he and 'Auntie' had developed an interdependence that seemed to serve them both well. By age nine, he was calling her 'Mother' to his friends outside his home and 'Auntie' to her face. David's progress through school was slow and he was regarded as limited, getting special tuition in opportunity classes for slow learners. At age 10, his case worker described him as a 'comforting, anxious, very appealing, slow, little boy who tries hard at school, works to capacity, plays hard, and spends a great deal of energy.'

David negotiated puberty comfortably with the support of his foster mother, asking about physiological changes and discussing with her the sex education movies he had seen at school. By 13 years of age, he was described as having developed sound values by his worker. Already compulsive in his behaviour, he readily adopted his foster mother's passion for neatness and cleanliness, showing perfectionist tendencies and adopting her prejudices. His case worker described him as 'rigid and fussy.' By 15 years of age he responded positively to his mother's increased control and the limits that she placed on his activity. He shopped with her, shovelled snow, papered rooms, and prepared meals for her when she was ill. They attended church together until he was 17, at which time he attended early mass alone, 'to get it over with.' By 18 years, he continued to share a dependent empathetic relationship with her: 'I am grateful to you Auntie, I really am. I think ahead, I hate to think of the time I will be alone. Are you ever lonesome, Auntie?' On his foster mother's part, the case worker observed, 'she understands him, loves him, bosses him, and seems to be letting up the strings.'

Throughout these adolescent years, David attended trade school and was fortunate in having three teachers whom he liked. They encouraged his skills, recognized his high motivation, and made him feel important. He was sometimes selected for open-house demonstrations. His capacity to attend to small details served him well, and he was described by one teacher as 'accurate, precise and logical in manipulating materials and reproducing design ... he used more logic in perceptual than in verbal problems. He enjoyed drafting, printing and woodworking.' However, on leaving school he accepted a job in a drug store, on the advice of his teacher. Here he remained for eight years, eventually managing supplies for three stores and going 'out on the road, setting up new stores and renovating old ones.'

Throughout his growing years, David received a very small allowance from his family which he savoured and spent carefully. He took on small jobs to earn pocket money and managed to save a considerable amount by the time he was 17. He adopted his foster mother's philosophy, 'work hard and save, and buy only what you need.'

David was consistently enthusiastic about boating, swimming, water-skiing, fishing, collecting frogs and insects, baseball, and bike riding. In the winter he adored hockey, sleigh riding, volleyball, Monopoly, and checkers. All these activities brought him into rewarding interactions with peers and adults. He related comfortably to others, a capacity that enabled him to enjoy the people he later met in his work.

By age 32, David's life had followed a conventional pattern. He had married a woman whom he described as 'understanding' and 'very, very good-hearted to get along with.' She had left work to remain at home to care for their son, now four years old, and baby daughter. She assumed the domestic and caretaking tasks, while he looked after the cars, home repairs, and renovations. David had adopted the strict, somewhat rigid attitudes of his 'auntie' toward his wife and children. He appeared to be the benign dictator, the breadwinner and disciplinarian. He assumed that he should be boss. When he and his wife argued, it was over 'little things' such as her doing something differently than he would: 'The odd time I'll give in and let her have her way.' He played with his son, read to him before bed ('most important'), took him to the park to play ball, went for walks together, put up a tent in the garden, and enjoyed other activities with him.

David and his family lived a somewhat isolated life, cut off from both his family and his wife's. Shortly after the birth of their son, his beloved 'auntie,' who delighted in his marriage and first child, died of pneumonia. His anguish at losing her was compounded by the shock and sense of rejection at having been left out of her will. Furthermore, his formerly supportive relatives, some of whom inherited her money, no longer made contact with him. However, David pulled himself together, stretched his finances, and bought the cottage that had brought him so much joy in earlier years. He put his many skills to use in renovating his house. Careful planning and budgeting allowed him to cope financially.

David left his job with the drug store chain because he felt the demands on him were increasing and he was not being appreciated. His new job, making fuse boxes, was providing him with satisfying promotions, but he regretted the competitive attitude of his co-workers (he had never liked competition, even as a child).

He had always gone to church, accepting it unquestionably as part of his life, and was planning a religious education for his children. He believed that the Church and its ideas had helped him in daily living. His outlook was pragmatic and lacked philosophical depth. He dealt with life as it came, adapting to what had to be.

At age 32, this warm-hearted, loving husband, father, and provider seemed surprisingly stable and emotionally healthy. His high standards ('If you can't do things right, don't bother with them') had created defences (he described himself as 'tense, jumpy, and having a short fuse'). His traumatic experience with his extended family had created some distrust and had made him cautious about being too open with people. However, he had many basic skills that made him feel confident about supporting his family. He felt that he had been loved by 'Auntie,' and that her acceptance and predictable values and rules had provided him with a happy, secure environment in his youth. These same values would now provide for his own family. David seemed resilient enough to recover from loss and disappointment. The most important thing was his family, a small world that he intended to protect.

David's coping skills were many faceted. This highly competent, somewhat brittle, controlling, striving, protecting, and overachieving young man was motivated by a set of values from his foster parent, and was later supported by his religion and an understanding wife. He had attained a level of functioning that had little relationship to his I.Q. His self-esteem came from developing work habits that were based on the same qualities he had displayed in school, and which had brought him early approval and recognition.

Darlene

In the first year of her life, Darlene was diagnosed by institutional workers as autistic: she demonstrated perseverative motor actions, passive responses unrelated to her environment, and a lack of affective response. At age 10 months Darlene's performance on the Gesell and Cattell scales revealed consistently dull-normal scores, both motor and verbal. She did not differentiate among her caretakers, passed her hands blankly in front of her face, and was tense and fearful, especially in boisterous play. The individual attention paid to her in her second institutional year appeared to elicit a happier, more outgoing attitude toward play, but she still lacked emotional response and rejected cuddling. At 19 months of age, Darlene's responsiveness had continued to increase with adult reassurance. She insisted on being clean and tidy, could say 'cookie' and 'ta ta,' and displayed aggressive behaviour about her toys.

As a result of this apparent progress, when she was 22 months old Darlene was placed in an adoptive home with an excitable, talkative mother, a quiet, loving father, and four sisters. The three older sisters made a fuss over her, while the youngest felt Darlene was a bit of a threat and bossed her around. Under this regime, Darlene became more venturesome and sought cuddling, especially if her 10-year-old sister was being cuddled. However, she was still cautious and prone to perseveration, e.g., repeatedly lacing her shoes. By age 34 months she had settled happily into her new home but was frightened of loud noises and withdrew if criticized. She often demonstrated compulsive posturing, and she picked at book corners.

By age three years, five months, Darlene scored mid-average on the Binet Intelligence Scale; her test performance was described as slow and cautious until she warmed up. Her play with other children was more assertive. She was sensitive and easily upset by harsh words. Some remnants of autistic behaviour (e.g., rubbing the backs of her hands in a circular motion on the table) prompted the tester to diagnose a degree of constitutional inadequacy, which would place her at greater risk for potential disturbance than the average child. Never interested in eating and constipated since birth, Darlene refused food; her mother, worried about nutrition and hating to see food wasted, began feeding her, a practice that she continued for many years and which later developed into a battle of wills.

At age four and one-half years, Darlene's comprehension and vocabulary had improved, and at age five she was reported to have a close relationship with her father (e.g., she ran to him for a cuddle when he got home, and liked to help him do jobs around the house) and was sensitive to how her mother felt (e.g., 'Are you mad at me, Mommie?'). But she did not play well alone and was considered by the case worker to be emotionally immature. She revealed her anxiety by nervous hand movements.

At age five years, 10 months Darlene's behaviours in a test situation swung from fearful and inhibited to free, laughing, and even silly. Her intellectual rating was in the low-normal range, and her speech was good; yet, she misunderstood the test instructions. Her fine motor control was poor. She saw male authority figures as overpowering and threatening, although she perceived maternal figures as pleasant.

At age seven, Darlene was reading, and had passed into Grade 2. Two months later, Darlene was daydreaming and distracting her classmates, and reported that she did not like school. Her teacher felt that firmness was required, and that Darlene was merely being stubborn. The case worker tried to convince the teacher that Darlene was timid and needed love. Darlene's final grades were a meagre pass, and she repeated Grade 2 to allow her time to mature emotionally and intellectually.

At age eight, Darlene's scores on intellectual functioning, language development, and eye–hand coordination were all low. She still revealed no sense of self and no capacity to relate to others; she still showed fear of male authority figures. She reacted to her world with passive dependence or withdrawal. She was described by her teacher as a 'walking shell.' 'She does everything beautifully, but she isn't there.' Her mother had to spell out her chores for her and remind her often. She ducked responsibility, and let others do things for her. She lost herself in daydreaming. As time went on, Darlene became increasingly remote, isolated from her environment, letting her mother nag and push her, and taking no initiative in her life. Her mother found it difficult 'to know what she is thinking or feeling': 'She doesn't open up and talk.' Her mother had to 'drag words out of her.' By the time Darlene was nine years of age, the school psychologist found her very withdrawn and unable to relate to the world. Darlene repeated Grade 3, earning As and Bs in a small classroom with a male teacher.

At various times in her childhood, Darlene's behaviour was described as 'passive,' 'unresponsive,' 'subdued,' 'frightened,' 'detached,' 'timid,' 'sulking,' 'shy,' 'vague,' 'moody,' 'superficial,' 'shallow,' 'gullible.' She was a 'non-participator in human events,' and was described as 'a living robot,' living in a fantasy world with 'no capacity to relate in a meaningful way,' and 'no self-concept, nor feeling for others in her world.' She was 'unreachable': one 'could speak to her two or three times with no response.' When spanked by her mother for being late, 'she did not shed a tear.'

Darlene appeared to drift through life passively, showing no self-direction and allowing herself to be regulated by her mother, who was thus manipulated into the role of making all decisions for her and of 'spoon feeding' her in day-to-day activities as well as literally, at meals. Her foster sisters described Darlene as 'not reacting to things or people like other children.' When she was 12 years old, a psychologist predicted that she would need constant direction at every step of her life – intellectually, emotionally, and socially – as she had no judgment. By age 15, Darlene's teachers, psychologists, and parents despaired of her ever living an independent life.

Darlene's interview at 27 years of age revealed that, in spite of pessimistic forecasts concerning her inability to succeed in the work world, she had successfully completed a commercial course that included hairdressing, general mathematics, science, merchandising, baking, mechanics, and millinery.

By age 20, Darlene had turned a part-time cashier's job at a drug store into a full-time position, which she kept for seven years because she 'enjoyed working with the public.' At age 25 she met her boyfriend, a pharmacy student apprenticing at the store. Shortly after this, a co-worker persuaded her to switch jobs and work in an office. Darlene missed the steady flow of people, and after 18 months seemed to lose interest in her work. Finally, she was fired for habitual tardiness.

At the time of her interview two months later, she had not seriously begun a job search nor had she considered retraining; she seemed disinterested. She was living in her own apartment and still had some money from her severance pay. Her voice was very weak and mild. When asked a question about her life or her beliefs, there would be a long silence; then, she would repeat the question as though such a thought had never occurred to her. Finally she would answer, 'Probably, I'd...'

Darlene reported that she tended to be a loner and avoided crowds and parties. She avoided all stress, drifting rather than taking control of her life. Surprisingly, she managed her finances well: she had never been on welfare, owned her own car, owed no money, and paid her credit card bills promptly.

Darlene had moved out of the family home without much forethought. She had heard of an apartment, went to see it, and got the keys all in one evening. 'If it [the process of apartment hunting] had dragged on, I would have talked myself out of it, which I do all the time ... Then I had to go and tell my parents.' Darlene said she had been thinking about moving out for several years but had actually gone apartment hunting only two or three times. She said her parents did not mind her moving out once the actual leave-taking was over and they realized it was done (in view of her past behaviour, it must have come as a shock). Darlene herself admitted to some second thoughts: 'It's quite a change – lonely sometimes.'

Darlene said she enjoyed dropping in on her parents and helping out around the house, which she did two or three times a week, even helping her mother mow and edge the lawn. She said they were on fairly good terms now: 'It's like a visit. I can get up and go home – it's a good feeling.' Her apartment was 20 minutes' drive from her parents' home, and they had visited her apartment once or twice in the five months she had lived there. Her mother still volunteered advice on what she should do, where she should go, what clothes she should wear, and how she spent her money: 'Sometimes they think I'm foolish.'

Although she resented taking her mother's advice, Darlene said that she would find it hard to go against her parents if they disapproved of her plans. She answered questions very slowly, admitting sometimes that she'd like to ask her parents what they thought.

Darlene said her parents liked her boyfriend, Al, and that he sometimes came with her to visit them, but not as often as she would have liked. Asked if she resented the fact that her parents made her feel guilty, she paused, then said, 'I don't know... [Pause.] I'm wrong no matter what! I'm still the baby in the family.' Still, at 27, tied to her parents for support and direction, Darlene nevertheless found the inner strength and motivation to move out on her own and gave the impression that while she did not in any way wish to break the tie with her family, neither did she have any yearning to return to live under their roof.

At age 27, Darlene appeared to be a bland, rather colourless young woman who functioned within a world that had been constricted by her early indifference to people and events. Although raised in a voluble, warm, upwardly mobile family where achievement and hard work were valued, she seemed to have remained on the periphery. She had been cajoled, protected, directed, and supported without demonstrating any overt response. She had neither appreciated nor fought this. As a result, she seemed to have very few internalized values. She had no desire to acquire money, either for spending or for saving. She seemed casual about future plans – marriage, job. She seemed mildly happy about her independent living arrangements. She had adopted her fiancé's religion without any serious convictions. She had no hobbies, no close friends except for her fiancé, and no apparent philosophy or plan for living. With so few inner resources, she gave the impression that she would be unable to survive traumatic events in her life unless supported by her immediate family.

Darlene's life adaptation was characterized by little self-direction. She drifted at the behest of events and people as they touched her life. Her actions reflected a poorly defined sense of self. Her habit of backing away from potential stress seemed a pattern of behaviour rather than a reaction to specific events. Lacking a hierarchy of values, her decisions were made with little conviction. She therefore did little long-term planning, drifting from day to day and from situation to situation. She rarely showed enthusiasm for anything.

Darlene's immature dependence on a benign and nurturing family had served her well, to date. With her best interests at heart, her parents had regulated, supported, and guided her life. They had also protected her from threatening circumstances. Whether Darlene could continue to function in her home and community would probably depend on the character of her fiancé and his willingness and ability to assume a controlling role in her life.

Although the course of Darlene's life adaptation indicated a particularly vulnerable young woman, she appeared, on the surface, to be an adequately functioning person. In her case, neither her early measured I.Q. nor her frail personality were accurate predictors of her adaptation at age 27.

Summary

Intellectual assessments of our subjects were undertaken when they were six, nine, 12, and 15 years of age. Early improvement in performance test scores, seen as the result of therapeutic interventions in the children's environment, gave rise to the question of whether adaptive patterns observed in school performance could predict successful work habits in the adults. Further, a correlation was hypothesized between I.Q. and successful adaptation in later life.

Phase III interviews failed to indicate a significant connection between either school performance or I.Q. and level of adult functioning. Other characteristics were found to account for adult competence, such as persistence, capacity for relationships, religious or philosophical convictions, and controlled anxiety in pursuit of goals.

8

The Invulnerable
Child: What Price?

Resiliency

Resilient children who resist the distorting effects of early adverse circumstances have long been identified in studies of normal human development such as the longitudinal University of California, Berkeley collaborative group.[1] However, it is only recently that this phenomenon has supplanted some of the previous preoccupation with maladaptive outcomes of early malign experiences. Since Bowlby's 1951 study on maternal deprivation[2] and its negative results, many reports have expanded our understanding of deprivation as a multi-dimensional condition. The plethora of attachment studies and Bowlby's monumental theoretical volumes have made us aware that mother–infant attachment is central to mental health. The focus on the negative effects of insecure attachments has heightened our awareness of the many dimensions of deprivation and helped us to recognize that attachments are formed not only to people but to objects, locations, and events.

It has been recognized that early psychoanalytic theory put spurious negative emphasis on the damaging effects of early non-nurturing experiences. This is not surprising, since many early studies were retrospective and clinical in nature, and reflected outcomes of a distressed and maladapted population. Countermanding this emphasis, the behaviourists in turn created an overly optimistic climate, with an em-

1 Jones, M.C., Bayley, N., MacFarlane, J.W., & Honzik, M.P. (Eds.) (1971).
  The course of human development. Waltham, MA: Xerox College Publishing.
2 Bowlby, J. (1951). *Maternal care and mental health.* Geneva: World Health
  Organization.

phasis on the powerful impact of benign parenting and education upon the future of children. In so doing, they failed to recognize the innate strengths and vulnerabilities of the human organism. Both points of view discounted temperamental orientations and innate individual differences.

By the 1970s, worldwide concentration on 'at risk' children spawned a multitude of studies that focused on early intervention. Such studies, frequently prompted by public policy, attempted to find ways of circumventing the impact of depriving environments on such children. Studies of 'at risk' populations tended to focus on vulnerable children. In response, such programs as Head Start were designed, evaluated, and modified over the next 20 years in an attempt to find ways to overcome the deficiencies in the lives of children who failed to fit into the social structure.

These studies persistently pointed to the fact that there were some resilient children who survived early damaging experiences regardless of intervention and became apparently well-adapted adults. Such children were labelled 'invulnerable.' By the 1970s interest in the phenomenon of resilient children spurred some reputable longitudinal studies[3] that focused on both the environmental and the constitutional factors that might account for later healthy adaptation.

By describing 'protective factors' that contributed to the well-being of 'invulnerable' children, researchers identified benign circumstances that modified or altered a potentially unhealthy adaptive pathway to maturity. Factors associated with well-adaptive maturity included: fewer than four children in a family; a minimum of two years between the birth of siblings; reliable early caretaking; limited parental workload; and a limited number of cumulative chronic stressful events while growing up.[4]

Rutter[5] furthered the understanding of resilient children by advocating an examination of processes. Rather than focus on 'risk variables' he developed the idea of a 'process of negotiating risk situations.' Hence,

3 Werner, E.E., & Smith, R.S. (1982). *Vulnerable but invincible.* Toronto: McGraw-Hill; Werner, E.E. (1985). Stress and protective factors in children's lives. In A.R. Nichol (Ed.), *Longitudinal studies in child psychology and psychiatry.* Chichester, U.K.: John Wiley & Sons; and Garmezy, N., & Rutter, M. (1989). *Stress, coping and development in children.* New York: McGraw-Hill.
4 Werner, E.E. (1985). Stress and protective factors in children's lives. In *Longitudinal studies in child psychology and psychiatry.*
5 Rutter, M. (1987, July). Psychological resilience and protective mechanisms. *American Journal of Orthopsychiatry, 57* (3).

he took the view that the key to understanding resilient children was found not in risk factors but in 'developmental and situational mechanisms involved in protective processes.' Resilience should not be viewed as a fixed attribute, but rather as a reaction to stressors that may change with changing circumstances. Hence, studies should focus, not on protective factors that enhance an individual's self-esteem, but on processes that protect an individual against risk mechanisms. Thus, protection is defined not as 'an evasion of risk but rather a mode of engagement with it.'[6]

Such insights helped us to understand the development of one of our subjects who could be termed 'invulnerable.' Tom's story contributed greatly to our knowledge of adaptive processes and resilient development arises. Analysis was made possible by the richness of the data collection until he reached age 29. Looking at Tom's life history, particularly his separation experiences and how he dealt with them, allowed us a glimpse of his pathway to his degree of mental health.

Tom

Tom spent the first six weeks of his life with his mother in a maternity home. At seven weeks of age, he was transferred to the institution where he was to remain for the next six years. When the rehabilitation program began, Tom was three years, four months old and was showing bizarre, compulsive behaviour, poor physical health, and the usual expected retardation in development. Over a period of three years, during which he received individual psychotherapy and lived in a therapeutic milieu, Tom emerged from a series of gains and regressions to a sufficiently healthy state that made home placement seem possible.

After 10 preliminary visits, Tom was placed in a foster family in which there were five siblings. Completely bewildered, he could not grasp the complexities of family life, and he was unable to accept his foster father. His incessant clinging to his foster mother perplexed and frightened her. She turned him outdoors for long, lonely periods of solitary play. With his dependency needs rejected, Tom at first tried to conform: 'Will you send me away if I don't like Daddy?' Finally, he turned to a fantasy world, in which he 'locked up bad people.' Fifteen months later, this sad, confused little boy was turned out of his foster home. The mother stated, 'Our home to Tom is *mother*, nothing else has any meaning.'

6 Rutter, M. (1987). Ibid.

In the recognition that family life was too socially complex for this lonely boy (now seven years, nine months old), the decision was made to place him in a warm, small country residence for children of limited capacity. Nature trails, animals, and outdoor activity were balanced by sound limits and routines that provided safe guidelines for children's behaviour. Initially, Tom continued to mourn the loss of his foster family, and when told that his mother was ill, asked, 'Is Mom so sick that she can't walk or cook? Will she die? Can I go back when she is better? I don't know any prayers to get her better. Does that mean that [this] is my home and I have no mother? Will I stay [here] until you find me another mom?' 'Will you find me a mom that will like little boys even when they are naughty?'

With the continued support of his case worker and an understanding and responsive environment, Tom eventually made a successful adaptation to this home, where he remained for a year. He no longer openly reverted to fantasies; he took an interest in the world around him, and showed sympathy and caring for some of the retarded children. On school entry at nine years of age, he found for the first time a warm, supportive teacher who encouraged his academic potential and took an interest in his appearance, his activities and feelings.

The improvement in Tom's well-being and his continuing request for 'parents of his own' prompted a move to a third placement, where the foster parents had seven children of their own. In spite of their past successes, this family faltered in dealing with Tom. His unusual behaviour frustrated the foster mother, who resorted to 'firmness and fear' as a way of controlling his immature demands: 'It repulses me to do up buttons and comb hair for a nine-year-old boy. I didn't do it for my children. I won't do it for him.'

Good fortune in finding his second sympathetic teacher compensated in school for some of the misery at home. His teacher sensed his fears of rejection: 'He is a sad child who desperately wants human warmth. He is not vague with me. He trusts me. He wants to talk to me a lot. He is starved. He is a likeable kid, kind and considerate. I have many chats with him to let him know he is a person. He is eager to learn – curious. No academic problems. He is the type of child who, if you ask what an object is, will tell you what it is for and then what it is. With peers, he is not ready for group activity.'

Eventually rejected by this foster family who believed he had a 'distorted mind,' Tom had to accept the decision of his case worker to move on to yet another unknown situation. Asked by his foster father,

'What would you like best of all?,' he replied, 'I would like to live in a volcano.' 'You can't live in a volcano.' 'Well, when it stops bubbling.'

Finally, a plan for placement emerged that was the most salutary of Tom's life. A summer on a farm was arranged with an active, warm-hearted, 63-year-old woman and her 70-year-old husband. Tom regarded them not as parents, but rather as Aunt Jenny and Uncle Bill. Eventually, Tom's case worker extended the placement to a more permanent basis. Aunt Jenny mothered Tom, and Tom responded: 'My mother is proud of me today.' Uncle Bill opened up the wonders of farm life and the joys of the outdoors. Once more, a sympathetic teacher in a country school became his mentor: 'He is an impatient, compulsive child, desperately in need of approval. He is accepted only by younger children and is very much a loner. He trusts no one with his possessions, coat, pencil or school books. I am very pleased with him. His vocabulary is remarkable. He uses it in the right context and knows what he is talking about.'

At home, Tom's joy in possessions was heart-warming. Every gift was fondled and protected. On receiving a steam engine after passing exams, he exclaimed, 'Thank you, thank you. I am so happy I can only say thank you. There's lots more I could say but it is all inside me and I can't make it come out!' During his twelfth year, Tom's healthy development continued with two expressed goals: 'to live with Aunt Jenny forever and ever, and to do well on exams!' At this time, his social maturity rating on the Vineland Maturity Scale indicated a nine-year level, and there was a heartening move to a more mature pattern on his security evaluation, from lower immature dependency (8%) to higher dependent trust (67%), reflected in higher expenditure of effort.

During his thirteenth and fourteenth year, Tom continued to entrench himself in his new family. Despite some pre-teen grumbling on his part, his foster mother was still attuned to him. Tom hugged Aunt Jenny, argued with her, and worried when she was not home. Uncle Bill thought the boy was 'great' and made no demands on him. Tom said, 'I really like Uncle Bill because he likes to teach me things and believes I can do things.' An assessment on the Wechsler Intelligence Scale showed considerable gain over the asssessment at nine years. Tom's strengths lay in the field of abstract reasoning, general information, and social comprehension. He demonstrated highly developed skill in verbal analysis and logical reasoning, though he was weak in conventional arithmetic. As his psychologist summarized, 'Tom's intellectual potential was far in advance of his fund of knowledge. He was a very bright lad who had incorporated information at an astonishing rate in view of his impoverished background.'

As Tom continued a more healthy maturational pattern, Aunt Jenny, now 67 years old, showed signs of declining health and an inability to cope with the argumentative, increasingly expansive adolescent she had sponsored. Uncle Bill was now deaf and withdrawn. Tom's need for more fuel for his active mind was still being met by an understanding teacher and the principal in the local school. Sensing rejection once more, he attempted to repress his needs and conform to Aunt Jenny's expectations, resulting in psychosomatic symptoms. In an attempt to maintain his relationship with Aunt Jenny, he became dependent and clinging, thus relinquishing some of his healthy self-trust and effort.

Tom's case worker arranged summer camp to relieve pressure on Aunt Jenny. By fall, a resident boys' school for 150 students seemed the only solution, fuelling the hope that Tom might still return home on weekends and holidays. This was not to be. Aunt Jenny became emotionally upset and unable to accept Tom's assertive behaviour. Long, lonely weekends ensued, which left Tom feeling as if he were living in a vacuum. When the final break came and Tom had to leave the home he had struggled to make his own, his response to the case worker's comment that 'life was not a bowl of cherries and he would have to be strong,' was: 'I feel sick all over when I think of Aunt Jenny. Life is a bowl of pits, and one has to dig very deep to find a luscious cherry.'

The following year in boarding school provided support for Tom's academic capabilities (Grade 9), and emotional support came in the form of weekends at the home of his case worker, or at his play therapist's home. Happily, good fortune was to shine again.

A young couple who had been directors at the camp Tom attended were captivated by this boy's sadness and earnestness and puckish sense of humour. They invited him for weekends with them in their country home. This relationship blossomed, and eventually they became his foster parents. The following two years were marked by increasing emotional stability and rewarding academic achievement. By 19 years of age, Tom felt part of this small family and was working toward marks which would gain him entry to university as a computer science major.

In a letter to his case worker Tom elaborated:

At school, the big question is complete. I hope that my interest will continue to expand. A teacher at present is working his butt off trying to get me a place in London so that I can once more sit in front of the big machine. New friends? Well, I am not pushing it but it is coming, and I will soon be like the rest of the people at school. This is a great house we are fixing up. Our big problem is hot water and central heating. We have two of the happiest dogs in the world. Soon we will be ready for you to visit us.

Tom's life seemed to be taking on the shape of 'normalcy.' The one weak aspect in his life was his inability to establish peer relationships. By the time Tom was 22 years old, he was studying computer science, had a baby brother to delight him, and was spending weekends and holidays with his 'family' and occasional visits to his case worker and his former play therapist. It appeared that his dependency needs were finally being met to a satisfactory degree and that his intellectual capabilities were flourishing.

Yet, such idyllic conditions were not to be for Tom. Midway through his second university year, he received word that his young foster mother had taken the baby and returned to her parents, leaving the foster father to remain in the home that they had renovated together. On returning home, Tom discovered that a new teenage foster child had usurped his place. No longer was there a congenial spot for him. Returning to university, he finished his year, leaning on casual acquaintances and seeking the support of staff for his academic progress. After this event, Tom seemed finally to relinquish his effort to find a 'family' for himself. Completing his computer training while living in university residences, he finally returned to Toronto, where he became successfully employed. He set up housekeeping in a simple downtown apartment which he furnished sparsely. There he remained until the time of his interview at age 29. This interview reflected predictable links to Tom's past and revealed a security profile of an intellectual, efficiently functioning young adult with repressed dependency needs. As such, he was prone to bouts of depression which, however, did not incapacitate him.

Fascinated by computers since high school days, Tom had obtained a job, immediately after graduation from university, in a large corporation where his knowledge was needed and where there were opportunities for advancement. Well paid and happy, he felt that his talents were recognized and rewarded. However, he made no lasting friendships in university or in his job. He was unable to cope with office politics. His abiding interest in computers filled his life, and his hobbies reflected his work interests. Living alone in a sparsely furnished, small apartment, Tom enjoyed experimenting with his personal computer. Intrigued by the scope and potential of modern technology, he planned to pursue his involvement in a 'Fourth Language Club,' which took computers into realms of communication beyond their generally accepted uses. His other two interests, short-wave radio and chess, likewise reflected the social distance with which he felt comfortable. His work and hobbies enabled him to demonstrate his competence and afforded him feelings of independent security.

Tom's emotional and social well-being were not so sturdy. He had no intimate friendships. He appeared never to have had a girlfriend his own age. He had a distant relationship with one male friend at work to whom he might have turned for collegial advice. He seemed to have abandoned his persistent longing for an immature dependent relationship by becoming part of a family by age 22.

His dependent relationships seemed to be of an immature nature, with the only two caring adults who still remained in his life – his case worker and his play therapist, both of whom he used for incidental advice, occasional meals, and visits on holidays such as Christmas. These adults, both more than twice his age, still provided him with support during rough times. However, when his difficulties had passed, he rarely contacted them, and it seemed never to have occurred to him that he might contribute something to their lives – for example, gifts or odd jobs. He actively avoided any situation that put social demands on him. He seemed to have learned the lesson that the social world had been so unpredictable that it no longer warranted his trust – hence his avoidance of peer relationships, either of a casual or an intimate nature.

Although he avoided organized religion, Tom had a philosophy for living. He doubted that 'there is a just God – a Supreme Being' who helped people live out their lives. He had met life's challenges, and anticipated doing so in the future, by relying on himself and what he had 'learned from his past experiences.' He would 'live each year as it came, hoping each experience would help him cope with the next.' On a more abstract level, he was not deterred by such threats as nuclear war because he perceived that increased knowledge would prevent a destructive war ('cool heads will prevail'). Hence, in the personal realm he coped by relying on his capacity to learn from past experience and on his intellect to rationalize the world's problems.

However, mere learning would not make him secure. He described his personal philosophy as 'a minimal cost strategy.' This young man, who when stressed as a child carried around small objects clutched in his hand and who 'locked bad people up so they couldn't get out,' was clinging to his money for 'safety.' He had no car, lived in a small apartment in a poor residential area, had neither debts nor credit cards, never bought on impulse, put minimal expense into clothing, and gave little away. He had no needs at the moment, and regarded himself as a good money manager. So Tom, whose vocation allowed him to feel independently secure and who earned a very good wage, was using his money, not to buy goods and services, but rather as a safety net (deputy agent) for the future. As long as his money held out, he would be 'O.K.'

Tom dealt with fears at many levels. Immediate anxieties were dealt with by withdrawal. Discouragement was 'walked away from.' Social inadequacies that aroused anxiety were dealt with by restricting social contact while continually building professional skills. Fear of death was dealt with by elaborate verbalization and hair-splitting speculations over how and when he might die, and what might happen 'after.'

Tom rarely demonstrated anger. Although he explained that he 'must be getting old,' it would appear that his carefully regulated life allowed for few annoying situations. When fear and anger were unavoidable and stress was prolonged, he repeated his lifelong pattern of demonstrating physical symptoms. Under extreme stress, he became depressed and suicidal. His happiest moments came from his identification with a scientific community. 'When that shuttle first went off – that was fantastic – all mankind got together – I've never been happier since.'

Tom's intellectual functioning was to him a great source of satisfaction and security. Despite his late entry into school at nine years of age, his intellectual assessments, at 10 years and at 14 years, indicated a remarkable vocabulary and strengths in abstract reasoning. By age 16, his symbolic thinking was 'precise and meaningful.' However, he was trying hard to control situations by 'elaborate verbalization,' which he used as a defence. During the interview at 29 years of age, he gave few short answers. He enjoyed, to an extreme, embellishing his responses, sometimes as a clever way of avoiding a direct answer. He best enjoyed thinking deeply about 'anything that will approach the "how" of the thinking process.'

In summary, Tom was a potentially vulnerable young man (see Table 4). Highly competent and intensely interested in one field of endeavour which offered an opportunity for enormous change and expansion in the future, he seemed well established and independently secure in vocational and avocational aspects of living. However, his trust in oth-

TABLE 4
Tom's security profile at age 29

	Independent Security (IS)	Mature Dependent Security (MDS)	Insecurity (I)	Immature Dependent Security (IDS)	Deputy Agents & Regression (DAR)
Family					
• parents					
• siblings					
Social relations					
• partner					
• general			x	x	
Vocation	x			x	x
Avocation	x				
Philosophy					
• money			x		x
• religion		x			
• health			x		
Emotions		x	x		x
Self	x	x		x	

ers was limited, and his skills in social relationships were minimal. His understanding of family life and the relationships within it was probably unrealistic. He seemed to have abandoned the effort to build and maintain social relationships.

His philosophic explanation of life on earth provided a satisfactory rationale within which he could feel relatively secure. However, in day-to-day living, he regarded the acquisition of money as his protection against future uncertainties.

Tom's sense of security was based in healthy competencies with respect to vocation and avocation. However, the dearth of interdependence with peers was potentially hazardous, as was his immature dependence on his two older 'friends,' who will be lost to him in the future.

His sense of self and his emotional well-being were tied to his relationship with his computer, over which he could exert total control. His identification with a scientific community seemed largely a fantasy, as it was not reciprocated by recognition by other 'scientists.'

TABLE 4
(*continued*)

___

Social relations
- No real peer friendships outside of work (Insecurity)
- One older person at work used for advice (Immature Dependent Security)
- Two longstanding 'friends' more than twice his age, who have provided intermittent psychological support, particularly in times of crisis (Immature Dependent Security)
- He has learned to use professional support (Immature Dependent Security)

Vocation
- Extremely competent and totally absorbed in the application of computers (Independent Security)
- Cannot cope with office politics (Deputy Agent)
- Asks elderly mentors about job change (Immature Dependent Security)

Avocation
- An extension of his interest in computers (Independent Security)
- Computer language club (Independent Security)
- Chess (Independent Security)

Philosophy
- Belongs to a scientific community (Mature Dependent Security)
- Notions have abstract intelligence (Mature Dependent Security)
- Miserly (Insecurity, Deputy Agent)
- Periods of depression (Insecurity)

Emotions
- Happy to be part of a scientific community (Mature Dependent Security)
- Fears intense emotion (Insecurity)
- Avoids emotion-arousing situations (Deputy Agent)

Self
- Relies on his computer – symbiotic relationship (Mature Dependent Security)
- Relies on routines (Immature Dependent Security)
- Always on time and no credit cards (Independent Security)

___

Thus, there was an unrealistic aspect to his sense of self that was potentially hazardous. His rigid reliance on routines and habits (always being on time, having no credit cards) indicated a somewhat brittle coping style.

Analysis of Tom's History

Looking back over the remarkable course of Tom's life, one wonders at his capacity for survival. Whether one adopts the view that 'protective factors' aided his adaptation or the more transactional notion of 'protective processes,'[7] one cannot disregard the possible role played by genetic make-up. Tom's unusual intellectual capability, which continued to blossom despite emotional trauma, was undoubtedly one of his greatest assets. His relatively good health, despite flare-ups of psychosomatic symptoms, had helped him carry on through major crises. He also revealed a capacity to relieve the dark side of life with occasional flashes of mischievous humour.

Rutter[8] discusses the notion that established habits, cognitive sets, and coping styles are mediating mechanisms that provide continuities to development by consolidating habitual ways of acting, which are both self-reinforcing and reinforced by others. These traits become internally organized through the development of cognitive sets about ourselves, our relationships, and our environment. Such habits, cognitive sets, and coping styles are viewed as mechanisms that not only perpetuate the same behaviours, but also, because of the consequences they create, have effects that might lead to other consequences and behaviours. In the first instance, they would perpetuate similar life trajectories; in the second, they would modify or change the original life trajectory. It is conceivable that Tom's cognitive style and competence created sufficient sense of self to contribute to his capacity to remain goal directed despite traumatic changes in his personal and social world.

A second notion of 'protective processes'[9] focuses on an explanation for differences in people's response to stress and adversity. Some succumb; some override it. We describe the latter condition as 'resilience.' Resilience is tied to the degree to which there is vulnerability or a protective process acting to modify an individual's response to a risky situation. The protective process represents factors that counter risk, particularly during key turning points in people's lives, at times a risk trajectory can be modified or redirected to a more adaptive path. Some of the protective processes that have salutary effects are those which reduce the perpetuation of negative chain reactions stemming from risk, and those which enhance self-esteem and self-confidence by the availability of secure and stable personal relationships.

7 Rutter, M. (1989). Pathways from childhood to adult life. *Journal of Psychology and Psychiatry, 30* (1), 23–51.
8 Ibid.
9 Garmezy, N., & Rutter, M. (1989). *Stress, coping and development in children.* New York: McGraw-Hill.

Close examination of Tom's emotional support systems would suggest that the stable presence of both his case worker and his play therapist provided the mediating process that facilitated his adaptation through each crisis and the intervals in between. The difficult decisions made by his case worker, in collaboration with the research team, were made in his best interest. No ideal placement was ever available, and it was the lot of his case worker to interpret to Tom the reasons for his many moves from one home to another. If Tom felt a sense of helplessness over his fate, this was not expressed to his case worker.

Expedience and luck also characterized Tom's life. The combined efforts of his case worker and his play therapist undoubtedly enabled Tom to be placed in his first home. After his placement, his play therapist seemed to have helped him work through his fears and hostility. Her incidental intervention, and his friendship with her family throughout his life, must have been a haven of warmth.

Overall, it appears that Tom's basic strengths, his coping strategies throughout traumatic experiences, his ability to attract helpful people and to accept their support, and the presence of two stable, older people in his life outweighed his negative experiences.

Tom's functioning at age 29 can be further understood by describing his developmental experiences in terms of continuities and discontinuities. Since one's definition of self is shaped by the interaction of the individual with a myriad of experiences from birth, each person's perception of seemingly shared events is unique. Who one is, and how one acts, depends on the psyche of each individual. Under normal circumstances, these experiences are shaped initially by family and its values. In time, the shaping widens to other families, neighbourhoods, school teachers, and other mentors. Most children experience a relatively consistent and related series of events that provide a continuous base on which to build the stepping stones of knowledge, values, beliefs, and habits. These are expressed in characteristic ways of acting and reacting, and can be observed in coping styles. The unexpected, fear-provoking, and unusual events in a child's life are usually mediated by a caring parent. Most children are sufficiently fortunate to take their developmental steps toward maturity without the threat of overwhelming trauma. Their interpretation of events is relatively benign.

It is tempting to speculate how Tom might deal with crises in the future. Has he the capacity for attachment and trusting relationships? Will he ever have the skills required for an intimate relationship? Would he have any capacity for parenting? Could he share his money and become more expansive in his lifestyle? What would happen should he be threatened by loss of his job? Has he learned skills in coping that will protect him against future disappointments? Is he bound forever to a constricted lifestyle and stifled emotional expression?

Summary

Resilience, or invulnerability, is the quality that best describes those children who are able to resist or overcome the deleterious effects of early deprivation. The factors here are manifold, and doubtless include environmental as well as genetic components – or, more likely, the interaction between the two. Thus, it is perhaps more useful to regard resilience as the outcome of processes rather than of specific protective factors.

9

The Group Profile:
How Healthy?

The information from our adult interviews was analysed using a similar methodology to that used when our subjects were 15 years of age. The framework of security theory, which had been maintained throughout the interviews, produced a format that permitted systematic recording and ordering of the data.

The information was useful in several ways. First, we looked for answers to the questions raised at age 15 through 18 regarding the children's residual immaturities at that time. Their social limitations with peers, and the immaturities evident in our subjects' conceptual thinking, had been regarded as the aftermath of their early deprivation, which had not been fully overcome. Could such deficits be overcome by continued maturation and learning? Furthermore, the subjects' immature dependency on their nuclear families was unusual for their age. To what degree would this behaviour permit a healthy emancipation as they moved into adulthood?

A second question asked of the data was, to what degree could this early-deprived group of subjects achieve mental health as adults? Although wide individual differences were to be expected, it was conceivable that the overall mental health of the group might reflect the degree to which the deficits due to severe deprivation were resistant to recovery.

A third matter of interest was the theoretical question of the extent to which mental health assets based on competencies and achievement in some aspects of function might compensate for deficits based on inadequacies and poor functioning in other dimensions of personality. For example, skills and success in vocational and avocational pursuits might have a 'halo effect' on an individual whose social skills were inadequate and for whom intimate relationships were elusive.

A fourth dimension to this analysis was directed to the definition of mental health. As we believed that mental health–or mental illness–is not a definitive syndrome but rather can be regarded as a balance created by a combination of healthy and less healthy factors, it was of interest to identify what might be the most healthy pattern of function, and which patterns might be deemed progressively less healthy. Would there be a way to distinguish among them?

Method

Categories in keeping with security theory were coded under the life area headings displayed earlier in Tables 3 and 4 and in Table 5, below:

TABLE 5
Grid for tabulating interview data

	Independent Security (IS)	Mature Dependent Security (MDS)	Insecurity (I)	Immature Dependent Security (IDS)	Deputy Agents & Regression (DAR)
Family • parents • siblings					
Social relations • partner • general					
Vocation					
Avocation					
Philosophy • money • religion • health					
Emotions					
Self					

Step 1: Tabulation of Data

Two raters familiar with security theory and with the interview format categorized behaviours from the records ($n = 20$ assessments).

1. Behaviour was deemed to demonstrate independent action. Acceptance of responsibility for one's actions was assigned to the category *Independent Security*. This applied for all life categories.
2. Similarly, behaviour that was deemed to demonstrate a sharing of decisions and their consequences with an intimate (peer) was assigned to the category *Mature Dependent Security*.
3. Behaviour that was deemed to indicate unresolved anxiety and indecision was placed in the category *Insecurity*.
4. Behaviours deemed to reflect a reliance on older or more authoritative persons to make one's decisions and to accept the consequences (responsibility) for them were assigned to the category *Immature Dependent Security*.
5. Behaviours deemed indicative of avoidance of decision making and avoidance of accepting consequences were assigned to the category *Deputy Agents and Regression*.

Twenty records covering each subject's lifespan were analysed in this fashion by each rater. Painstaking notations of all behaviours were rated and listed according to categories The ratings were then compared to assess the level of agreement between the raters. Whenever there was disagreement, the differences were discussed until agreement was reached. The two raters eventually were able to agree on all categories on each record.

Having completed this stage of tabulation, the raters developed a second record to tabulate the frequency of the appearance of the categorized behaviours. By totalling the tabulations, they discovered patterns of behaviours that reflected the mechanisms by which each individual coped with life events. Both individual and group patterns emerged.

A predominance of adaptive coping strategies of independently secure and maturely dependent secure nature was considered a reflection of good mental health. Some deputy-agent and regressive mechanisms were expected to be present in a healthy pattern as necessary ways of masking transient insecurities arising from insurmountable life difficulties. These mechanisms, however, should not predominate in a healthy individual.

Step II: Group Data Summary According to Life Areas

1. Examination of the social adjustment of our twenty subjects re-
    vealed a healthy overall adaptation. Fourteen subjects have had re-
    ciprocal friendships with people on whom they could rely to share
    decisions and responsibilities. Of these, 10 were spousal relation-
    ships. However, there was one exception to the healthy reciprocal
    spouse relationship insofar as one female subject seemed highly
    insecure and clung to her husband in an infantile relationship.

    In regard to group activities such as parties, crowds, or unfamil-
    iar social settings, our subjects seemed less healthy. Fourteen felt
    insecure in groups. Of those that felt more comfortable in this kind
    of setting, four covered up feelings of inadequacy by using deputy
    agents.

2. Examining the data from the point of view of self-concept and self-
    esteem revealed that over half (12) the subjects had a strong sense
    of self, based on a capacity to act independently, and they also had
    a feeling of confidence in their own decisions. Two others seemed
    to need the support of a reciprocal peer relationship to feel confi-
    dent in themselves. The remaining six used deputy agents and im-
    mature dependence to bolster a seemingly inadequate sense of
    self.

3. An examination of vocational and avocational skills revealed that
    all but two subjects were independently secure. They had hobbies
    and interests other than job-related ones. The remaining two
    seemed to lack clear direction to their work-related lives. All sub-
    jects but three (i.e., 17) were coping with their finances very suc-
    cessfully, although of the copers, three felt financially insecure. Of
    the three non-copers, one was receiving unemployment insurance
    and two were on welfare. In the past, three of the subjects, now in-
    dependent, had been on welfare at least once, and four had been
    on unemployment insurance. Hence, the majority of subjects were
    at that time supporting themselves and their families as well as
    making a contribution to their community.

4. With regard to their nuclear families, 11 of the 20 subjects were
    comfortably emancipated and enjoyed a reciprocal interrelation-
    ship with them. Four never seemed to achieve independence from
    their families, but believed they shared a reciprocal relationship.

Eight of the emancipated subjects felt insecure about their families, and their family relationship was supported by the use of deputy agents and immature dependence. Twelve of the subjects had a maturely dependent relationship with their siblings.

5. Concerning the subjects' attitudes toward their health, 10 of the 20 felt they were maintaining their health wisely, and six employed deputy agents to mask their anxiety about their health. Only one expected someone else to take responsibility for her health.

6. The belief in some philosophy of life to help ponder unanswerable questions was considered a necessary quality for mental health. One aspect of this could be religious faith. It appeared that nine of our 20 subjects had achieved this level of thought. Twelve of the group had an immature dependent faith in a guiding religious dogma that offered them comfort. Of these, five enriched their belief with additional philosophies arising from their own speculation. Five of the group were without the comfort of religion or philosophy to ameliorate anxiety, and these subjects felt insecure about the purpose of their life and their future.

As a group, our subjects had overcome early social deficits, most having intimate peer relationships. However, most of them felt discomfort in groups. They were unusually competent in vocational and avocational pursuits, and many of them had a philosophy or religious belief to sustain them. They were, on the whole, a remarkably secure group of young adults.

Individual Profiles

While it was interesting to examine the level of security of the group as a whole, an examination of individual patterns of security proved the most useful way of applying the theoretical framework. Used as a clinical tool to establish the degree to which each individual was coping with life and by which mechanisms, this framework allowed an evaluation of present mental health and a prognosis as to future coping skills. For example, a mental health profile of George (the 'watcher' discussed in Chapter 3) exemplified a particularly healthy young adult. At 15 years of age, George had many assets that pointed to a healthy future.

George

Having completed a degree in psychology, George at age 30 was successfully employed in a job associated with his training and for which he was well paid (IS). He was an attractive, friendly, enthusiastic man (IS), married to a woman who shared many of his goals, and he was determined that his marriage would work (MDS). He owned his house and a car and had few other debts (IS). He had maintained a comfortable relationship with his family – one of apparent mutual respect and support (MDS). He had maintained a religious affiliation, and had a philosophic orientation to life (MDS). He had both intimate and extended friendships, and did regular volunteer work in the community (MDS). A judgment of his mental health in adulthood showed a continuation of his early healthy adaptation at age 15. His profile (see Table 6) displays an unusual degree of independent and mature dependent security and a dearth of defensive behaviours.

Such a mental health profile is a highly desirable one, indicating a young man depending on skills and mutual relationships for maintenance of his mental health. This profile points to a realistic and adaptive approach to life that requires little or no reliance on defensive mechanisms to mask insecurity. Just as we were able to predict at 15 and 18 years of age that George was likely to continue to develop and maintain healthy coping strategies, we believe that it is possible to project ahead from age 30. George is likely to continue to live his life by facing its challenges in a mentally healthy way.

Maurice

Another example of a mentally healthy young adult is Maurice, whose history was also discussed in Chapter 3. Although more vulnerable than George, Maurice had found satisfactory coping skills, countered by immature dependence and defence mechanisms. His security profile (see Table 7) was not as well defined as George's.

Maurice's mental health at age 27 reflected an unusual pattern of development and extreme life trauma. As the result of consistent difficulties with peers during his early years, a disability that lasted until he graduated from high school, Maurice had been encouraged to develop his mechanical skills. As a result, he had become proficient in electronics, and also was a very capable 'jack of all trades.' By the time he

TABLE 6
George's security profile at age 30

	Independent Security (IS)	Mature Dependent Security (MDS)	Insecurity (I)	Immature Dependent Security (IDS)	Deputy Agents & Regression (DAR)
Family					
• parents		x			
• siblings		x			
Social relations					
• partner		x	x		
• general		x	x		
Vocation	x				
Avocation	x				
Philosophy					
• money	x				
• religion		x			
• health		x			
Emotions	x				
Self	x				

was 27 years of age, he was completely confident in his ability to make a living (IS). Although he was not working at the time of the interview, he displayed no concern regarding a future job. Maurice's work skills had provided a means of consolidating the friendships that had eluded him in early youth. However, as yet Maurice had not had a close relationship with a girlfriend or other intimate (I).

As a result of Maurice's supportive and loving relationship with his adoptive family, he had found a clear definition of self (IS) through identification with them. Although both parents had died within a week of each other when Maurice was 23 years old, he had inherited their estate, continued their traditions, and was proud of his nuclear family, including his 103-year-old grandmother (MDS). However, he regretted

TABLE 7
Maurice's security profile at age 27

	Independent Security (IS)	Mature Dependent Security (MDS)	Insecurity (I)	Immature Dependent Security (IDS)	Deputy Agents & Regression (DAR)
Family					
• parents	x	x	x		
• siblings					
Social relations					
• partner					
• general		x			
Vocation	x				
Avocation	x				
Philosophy					
• money	x				
• religion		x		x	x
• health	x				
Emotions	x				
Self	x				

the fact that his extended family of aunts, uncles, and cousins had ignored him after the death of his parents (I) and that he had little to do with them at present.

Maurice felt that 'God' and religion had pulled him through the crises of his parents' deaths (IDS). He routinely went to church. At the same time Maurice, made his world seem safer by belief in such superstitions as avoiding 'unlucky' numbers, black cats, and making important decisions on 'Friday the thirteenth' (DAR).

With regard to money, Maurice had been wise, investing the proceeds of his family estate in a house and van (IS) and doing renovations as a hobby while increasing the value of his investments (IS). He had learned to deal with his emotions in a satisfactorily controlled way and was careful about his health (IS).

Maurice's security profile demonstrated a healthy picture, with only two areas of vulnerability: the fact that he was isolated from his extended family, and that he had found no intimate supportive relationship yet. However, one would anticipate a continuation of healthy functioning in the future, based on his past capacity for emotional and social growth and his present skills and assets.

David

Another security profile, that of David (see Chapter 7) demonstrated an even more vulnerable security status. David had considerable coping strength based on a variety of independent skills and strong mature dependencies. However, persistent anxieties that were dealt with using chronic deputy agents weakened the picture. His security status at age 31 had been achieved in the face of many difficulties throughout his life. Limited intellectual ability, matched by poor school achievement, was compensated for by tremendous persistence and a will to achieve. As a result, he developed trade skills and eventually assumed managerial jobs, which he carried out with apparent success. Fostered by older parents (the father dying 18 months after foster placement), David was reared by a single mother who insisted that he call her 'Auntie.' Although adoption was denied him, he later assumed the family name to confirm his identity with it. Despite this arm's-length stance, his foster mother was attentive to David's welfare, and they seemed to have a mutually supportive 'partnership' as he matured. David's sorrow at 'Auntie's' death was followed by the shock of being left out of her will. The subsequent abandonment by his extended family deepened his sense of hurt and isolation. His supportive wife and his concern for his young family helped him through this crisis.

David's security profile (see Table 8) reflects the satisfactory trade skills that ensured him well-paid jobs, an opportunity for change, and promotions (IS). However, he was overly sensitive to criticism and disliked competition (I). Furthermore, he liked to be 'in charge.' (DAR). He treated his wife and two children in an old-fashioned, authoritative way (IS). He cherished his memories of 'Auntie' and of the family cottage, which he bought after her death and renovated for his own family (MDS). Yet, he was deeply hurt by being left out of 'Auntie's' will, and felt betrayed by his extended family him (I). His general approach to social situations was to conform to the rules (MDS). He enjoyed meeting new people (IS), but was slow to put his trust in them (DAR).

TABLE 8
David's security profile at age 31

	Independent Security (IS)	Mature Dependent Security (MDS)	Insecurity (I)	Immature Dependent Security (IDS)	Deputy Agents & Regression (DAR)
Family					
• parents	x	x	x		
• siblings					
Social relations					
• partner			x		
• general	x	x		x	x
Vocation	x		x		x
Avocation	x				x
Philosophy					
• money	x		x		
• religion				x	
• health	x				
Emotions			x		x
Self	x				

David and his young family went to church regularly and accepted the discipline and dogma of the Church (IDS). He felt that religion helped in daily life (MDS). David's skilful management of money enabled him to buy a house and two cars. He believed in hard work and in buying only what he needed (IS). He had a fear of carrying debt (I). He enjoyed his hobbies, most of which were carrying out jobs in his house (IS). However, he was a perfectionist (DA), and these tendencies made him put great demands on himself, resulting in compulsive behaviour and a 'short fuse.' He seemed rather volatile and somewhat fearful (I). His pragmatic acceptance of what life brings, dealing with it and moving on, was a satisfactory coping strategy (IS). He took care of his health by consistent attention to it (IS).

TABLE 9
Frank's security profile at age 30

	Independent Security (IS)	Mature Dependent Security (MDS)	Insecurity (I)	Immature Dependent Security (IDS)	Deputy Agents & Regression (DAR)
Family					
• parents				x	x
• siblings		x			
Social relations					
• partner			x		
• general		x			
Vocation			x	x	x
Avocation	x	x			
Philosophy					
• money				x	x
• religion		x			
• health	x				
Emotions		x		x	x
Self		x			x

Frank

Finally, we examine the profile of Frank, a 30-year-old man whose mental health seemed to be considerably more fragile than that of the last three (see Table 9). Reared in an adoptive home with his biological sibling, Frank had the good fortune to have acquired attentive, considerate, warm parents. He had trouble settling into a vocation owing to unrealistic expectations in relation to his skills. As a result, Frank had 10 jobs in eight years, none of which lasted longer than two and a half years (DAR). He had no special skills, and had completed only Grade 12 (I). Despite this, he masked his insecurity by a show of confidence, quitting jobs because he felt poorly paid, and venturing into new businesses because he believed he was better than he was (DA). During his intervals between jobs he had lived on unemployment insurance (IDS), and when setting up a new venture, he believed that it was appropriate to invest in costly photography equipment because his parents would pay for it (IDS). At age 30, Frank still lived with his parents, who supported him between jobs. Yet, Frank resented their control over him and their occasional disapproval (DAR). He had a comfortable group of extended friends including his brother and sister, all of whom attended school together (MDS). He was still comfortable with his family, feeling firmly embedded in it. Family activities were warm, and there was a good feeling among siblings (MDS). Frank had a distant relationship with his girlfriend, who lived 'out of town' (DAR). He claimed to be looking still for a 'girl who cares' (I).

Frank believed in God and went to church every Sunday. His faith helped him through the death of a friend (MDS). He looked after his health, and belonged to organizations that promoted health (IS). He at one time took a course in mountain climbing (IS). In contrast to this healthy outlook, Frank had abysmal skills in the making and management of money, relying on his parents to support him financially when he quit a job or ran out of unemployment insurance.

It appeared that Frank was an immature young man, lacking basic skills and confidence while masking his insecure feelings by boasting. He still remained dependent on his family for financial and emotional support and felt most comfortable when engaging in activities that included other people. He had yet to find an intimate partner with whom to share his life. This essentially unhealthy picture was countered by his genuine affection for and investment in his family life, his group of friends, and his church. He was not yet ready to face life's challenges on his own and therefore was vulnerable to his insecurities. In fact, it appeared that Frank was one of the few children in our study who did not emerge from the immaturities that were evident at ages 15 through 18. Should Frank ever gain confidence by success in a vocation, he might feel sufficiently secure to take the next step in his maturation by emancipating himself from his immature dependency on his family. One wonders, how he would fare were his parents to become unable to provide him with money and shelter.

Summary

Security theory is a useful framework by which to judge the behaviour of an individual, as it mirrors emotional well-being, or mental health.

Viewing mental health as a continuum reflecting an ever-shifting, balance of factors avoids the rigidity of a diagnosis of illness or, at the other end of the spectrum, an unrealistic expectation of a constant state of emotional well-being. Emotional states shift from healthy to less healthy, depending on complex events throughout the lifespan. The choices made by an individual in minor or major crises both reflect and create that person's emotional state. According to security theory, those choices which reflect independent decisions and the taking of responsibility, or those which are shared with a contemporary, are the healthiest choices. Indeed, the habit of making choices reflects a healthy approach to living, because it encourages the development of skills and the facing and solving of problems. Avoidance of problems and decisions not only reflects insecurity but creates and enhances it. Procrastination, 'sour grapes,' lying, and non-participation are some of the deputy agents used in such unhealthy strategies.

The balance of factors that reflect healthy coping strategies can be depicted graphically, as illustrated by the subjects in our study. Only a portion of our group is represented here. Each profile was different and reflected the subject's emotional well-being at a single point along the lifespan. Each profile demonstrated the habitual patterns of choices and uses of support employed by each subject to maintain emotional well-being. It seems reasonable to assume that the patterns displayed by a subject at age 30 indicate future patterns of behaviour. However, life-jarring traumas might dislocate a person's usual pattern of functioning.

Security theory assumes that the individual actively steers his or her course in life. It resembles the notion of Piaget, that an organism actively seeks out stimuli and makes choices that enhance its potential for optimal growth. Rutter's understanding of resilience similarly emphasizes the individual's approach to 'negotiating risk situations.' Thus, one should engage oneself in risk situations rather than evade them. Security theory likewise attaches importance to the making of choices.

10

Where Are the Others?
A Study of a
Contrast Group

As the adult interviews were proceeding on our long-term study (phase III; 1987), we wondered what had happened to a residual group of children who had the same institutional beginnings but whose journey to maturity had taken a different route. When our study began (1955–56) there were 85 children living in the institution. Twenty-two of these children who had been exposed to the initial therapeutic program were later moved on to traditional foster care under the supervision of the Catholic Children's Aid Society (CCAS). Records of these children's lives would have been accumulated and stored by that agency.

By 1987, many early-deprived children continued to reach maturity demonstrating severe maladaptive behaviours. Some of the most visible children were wards of the state who were under the supervision of child care agencies. These children were the recipients of repeated psychological assessments and much social work practice. Good intentions abounded. How did the system fail these children? Did practical considerations take precedence over the best interests of the child? Were agencies unwittingly structured to accommodate the cababilities of administrators and case workers rather than to serve their clients? Were government policies really serving the best interests of such children?

By this time, we had come to believe that successive life events were more powerful moulders of later adaptation than early experiences. We wondered how the histories of those 22 children would compare with those of our study group, since both had similar early backgrounds. What would be the adaptation of the contrast group on reaching maturity? Would their life experiences explain, to any degree, such adaptation?

Tracing the Subjects

When our adult interviews were concluding in 1987, the coordinator of psychological services at the CCAS undertook a search of this group's records. There was concern that many foster children were not benefiting from the recommendations of the professional staff, as they kept reappearing for clinical evaluations. The task of tracing these children proved unexpectedly time consuming and frustrating. Records, stored on microfiche, were difficult to access. Sporadic notations by ever-changing social workers reflected the discontinuities in many of the children's lives. As a result of changes of homes, and changes in case workers, some of the children appeared to have lost a personal identity. For this reason, records of only 14 of the 22 children could be selected for analysis. Only these records appeared to have sufficient data to warrant follow-up, as they seemed to reflect fairly consistent contacts from the early lives of these children to the age of majority (18 years), when they were discharged from the custody of the CCAS. Twelve of the children were male and two were female.

The long-term information on even these 14 children, when contrasted with our original study group, was fraught with inadequacies. Long gaps of time between notations frequently occurred, with sporadic and sometimes vigorous notations at times of crisis or when the children were in transition. The multiplicity of case workers responsible for the children as they became the unwitting victims of custodial decisions was reflected in sometimes contradictory comments about the children's adaptation to their experiences. One felt at times that the point of view of the various case workers took precedence over the essence of the child. Finally, there was great unevenness in the amount of information available from child to child, thus making comparisons difficult. Regrettably, in some instances, the notations on the children's behaviour indicated underlying emotional distress that remained both unacknowledged and untreated. Reasons for this were difficult to identify.

When this second investigation was begun, we anticipated evaluating data that lent themselves to quantification – for example, the length of time the children spent in institutional care, the number of changes of home, the number of case workers involved, and the significant people in the children's lives. Such a pursuit proved troublesome. Even more challenging was the attempt to evaluate the subjects' mental health at the time of their discharge, or to project the quality of their future functioning in the community. The educational status, motivation, and self-image of these children remained obscure. From the limited case notes, it was difficult to evoke an image of the subject as a person. The criteria believed to create a mentally healthy individual and which had been used for our major long-term study (i.e., the capacity to form healthy attachments, and the ability to achieve reciprocal mature dependencies accompanied by independent capabilities) were difficult to assess from such meagre data.

The number of placements was regarded as a critical factor in the children's capacity to function satisfactorily in late adolescence. Here, there was great variability. The number of placements ranged from two to 21. Yet, first examination of the histories seemed to reveal no substantial link to later adaptation. The length of placement and quality of care were also deemed to be important to later successful adaptation: the assumption was that the longer the placement, the deeper would be the attachment between the child and the foster family. However, only quality of care seemed to be reflected in later adaptation, with poor quality seemingly more powerful in outcomes than good quality care. Further, only three and possibly four of the 14 children experienced what could be considered excellent care.

Our original intent to describe these children as a group was thus thwarted. No pattern emerged that seemed common to all. Faced with these data, we were forced to report most of our findings in the form of individual histories. In so doing, we were compelled to contemplate the position of a child in the custody of an agency that attempts to provide substitute care in the absence of biological family.

The Child in Care

Children living in foster homes are extremely vulnerable: emotionally, they 'belong' to no one. The substitute parenting offered by foster parents is intended as a replacement for that of a child's biological parents. Ideally, good care includes offering a child emotional support, an opportunity for attachment to caring adults, and the experience of family life through which to absorb a system of values and respect for the rules of communal life. The opportunity to attend schools in a stable community, to develop friendships, and to anticipate the future rewards of education provide additional normalizing experiences for foster children. In reality, a perfect match of child with foster family is difficult to achieve. When biological children clash with their parents, the family rarely considers 'giving up' on the relationship. For the foster child, the prospect of being 'given up' is always present.

Adding to the child's vulnerability is the omnipresence of a case worker who takes the ultimate responsibility for major decisions regarding the child's 'disposal.' If one foster home doesn't work out – what next? Again, under ideal conditions, a child is not just another problem in a heavy caseload, but rather, a person with whom the case worker has become familiar. Hopefully, a child in foster care should not have to deal with the additional anxiety of appeasing significant persons who make decisions about his or her welfare. How must such a child feel when a continuous series of workers and foster parents becomes the normal expectation in life? Who accepts the child's sorrows, disappointments, and anger? Can the child ever develop a sense of power over his or her own destiny?

Tabulation of the Data

Table 10 illustrates the number of placements and number of case workers in each child's life from time of placement with the agency to age of majority. This table does not indicate the duration of placements, i.e., a child may have experienced several placements in a short period and then remained for a long time in one home.

As can be seen, no child had fewer than two homes from infancy to age of majority. Two children had 21 different homes; one child had 13 and two others experienced nine. Four children had only five different placements; three had four homes. Only one child had two homes, and another only three.

More dramatic than changes in homes was the multiplicity of case workers who passed through these children's lives. One child was supervised by 21 workers; another had 17, and four others had 15. The smallest number of workers experienced by one child was seven; the next smallest was 10, while two others had 11. There was great variation in the patterns: one of the children who experienced 21 placements had 21 case workers also. Another, presumably more fortunate, child who had 21 placements, was supervised throughout these changes by 10 workers. One child, more favoured by having only two placements, experienced seven different case workers, while another child had only three placements but was under the supervision of 15 different workers. Three children having only four different homes had a range from 11 through 17 case workers.

TABLE 10
Numbers of placements and numbers of case workers per subject to age 18 years

Subject	1	2	3	4	5	6	7	8	9	10	11	12	13	14	15	16	17	18	19	20	21
A	×o	×o	×o	×o	×o	×o	×o	×o	×o	×o	×o	×o	×o	×o	×o	×o	×o	×o	×o	×o	×o
B	×o	×o	×o	×o	×o	×o	×o	×o	×o	×o	×	×	×	×	×	×	×	×	×	×	×
C	×o	×o	×o	×o	×o	×o	×o	×o	×o	×o	×o	×o	×o	×o	o						
D	×o	×o	×o	×o	×o	×o	×o	×o	×o	o	o	o	o	o	o						
E	×o	×o	×o	×o	×o	×o	×o	×o	×o	o	o										
F	×o	×o	×o	×o	×o	o	o	o	o	o	o	o	o	o	o						
G	×o	×o	×o	×o	×o	o	o	o	o	o	o	o	o	o							
H	×o	×o	×o	×o	×o	o	o	o	o	o	o										
I	×o	×o	×o	×o	o	o	o	o	o	o	o	o	o	o							
J	×o	×o	×o	×o	o	o	o	o	o	o	o										
K	×o	×o	×o	×o	o	o	o	o	o	o	o	o	o	o							
L	×o	×o	×o	×o	o	o	o	o	o	o	o	o	o	o	o	o	o				
M	×o	×o	o	o	o	o	o	o	o	o	o	o	o	o	o	o					
N	×o	×o	o	o	o	o	o														

x = no. of placements   o = no. of workers

Examination of these data demonstrated that discontinuity was the norm in these children's lives. Continuity was elusive. Opportunities for attachment were compromised. Judged by the criteria of our major study, these maturing young people looked very frail. Owing to the lack of substantial data, one can only hypothesize about their mental health as adults. Would they sustain compassionate partnerships? If they were to become parents, what degree of emotional support and caring control would they offer their children? Would they be able to maintain a job? Would they have religious or philosophic beliefs to sustain them through difficult times? From what sources had they formed their values?

Keith

Keith's history illustrates the difficulties of isolating critical factors in the experiences of these children. He was fortunate in having found both a relatively long-term placement and excellent, consistent care by the time he was five and one-half years old. However, by that time he had experienced 10 different placements. These previous placements had included three foster homes, one adoption-probation placement which collapsed within two months, one return to his natural parents, and four institutional placements. When he finally obtained a long-term placement with this family, there were already two older adopted children who were well established.

Keith presented many problems. Despite this, his foster family provided him with excellent, consistent, and loving care, and he made remarkable progress over the next few years. However, as he entered his teens, he began to have problems at school, and was said to be lying and stealing. His foster parents complained that he was irresponsible and absent-minded, and they began to request help for him. This, unfortunately, was not made available, but they continued to maintain him in their home. A case worker noted that Keith might be sensitive to the fact that the two older children were adopted, whereas he remained in foster care. This situation had not been explained satisfactorily to him. He began to challenge his parents' values and discipline. As his behaviour put more stress upon the family, they again sought professional assistance from the agency, and for reasons not clear in the case notes, their request was turned down.

The decision was made to remove Keith from his foster home. No therapeutic mechanisms were set up for him or the family, and once again he experienced a series of short-term placements. At one stage, the long-term foster family considered taking him back on condition that therapy be established. This was denied. Keith became increasingly alienated, and all contact with his long-term foster family was cut off. At his discharge at the age of majority, he was described as living independently, employed, but alienated from his peers. He had achieved only a Grade 9 education.

Keith's attitudes, feelings of self-worth, emotional state, and educational competence at the time of discharge could not be evaluated. Unlike many of these children, he had the good fortune to be cared for by a family who were ready for a long-term commitment, a factor that should have worked in his favour. Was his inability to trust himself or others a result of the agency's failure to provide sufficient support for his foster family? Did his lack of trust reflect the failure of his case workers to interpret his insecurities and mediate the breakdown between Keith and his foster family? Or, was his mistrust a reflection of the 10 previous chaotic transitions in his life? Reading Keith's history evokes a sense of his alienation from family and peers, as well as a predominance of insecurities that overpowered the influence of more stable experiences.

Jamie

Given the difficulties of finding foster families who are committed to offering long-term care, it was heartening to find that 13 of the 14 children in the contrast group had experienced at least one long-term placement. The duration ranged from five to 16 years and averaged eight years. The one subject who experienced no long-term foster placements was Jamie, who spent eight and one-half years in institutional settings and had 14 moves until the age of discharge at age 18. None of these placements, with the exception of his early institutionalization, lasted longer than two years, six months.

Jamie had been placed in the Neil McNeil home a few weeks after birth and shortly thereafter became a Crown ward. Here there was ample notation. His first two years prior to the rehabilitation program were characterized by extreme developmental delay and peculiar mannerisms for which he had a neurological examination. He was regarded as 'physically healthy, but mentally slow,' and foster care was recommended. In the absence of a home, Jamie remained in the now rehabilitated institution for the next two years, developing behaviour problems that prompted an assessment for autism. The reasons given for this referral were 'abnormal fearfulness, difficulty in getting along with other children, inability to make choices, temper tantrums, aggressive and violent behaviour, delayed social development and immature speech.' Attempts to take him from the institution for pleasure outings resulted in sudden outbursts of fear and anxiety – kicking, biting, and clawing, followed by dejection and remorse.

After Jamie had spent three weeks in a treatment centre, his case worker noted some improvement: 'His vocabulary was better, still using gestures, but in much more communicative ways. His anxiety appeared to lessen, but he was terrified by dogs and even minor hurts, and became disorganized and impatient if he experienced difficulty with play equipment.' It had also been noted that Jamie had 'feminine' mannerisms. As the months passed, and he returned to the institution, further improvement was noted. Following his fourth birthday, Jamie continued to live in a small, protected unit in the institution with a unit housemother and two other children – a controlled, secure setting. His need for constant adult attention and direction was evident. Any attempt to expand his world presented difficulty – he became confused, disorganized, and demanding. If his wishes were denied, he usually demanded 'to sit on the adult's knee, almost compulsively embracing and kissing that person.' Under this regime, Jamie showed continued improvement, but as he approached his sixth birthday, and no foster home could be found for him, a placement in another institution seemed inevitable. At the age of six years, three months, he was moved. Although his adjustment was slow over the following months, he gradually accepted the new setting.

Three years later, the professional staff decided Jamie was ready for a foster home. At the age of nine and one-half years, he went to his first foster family. Adaptation to family life proved overwhelming for Jamie. He rejected his foster father, and his behaviour was difficult for the family to understand. Eight months later, he was returned to the institution, where he declared that he disliked group living and wanted a home. He was generally irritating to both staff and children. Another home was found for him with experienced foster parents. The foster mother, having worked as a unit housemother, knew Jamie, and welcomed him to their home. He adjusted reasonably well, although his foster mother found his constant demands trying. He seemed to form a comfortable relationship with his foster father and shared family chores with him. There was some competitive behaviour between Jamie and his younger sister, who was handicapped, but on the whole their relationship was positive. However, all was not well. After six months in his foster home, Jamie's foster mother requested his removal, finding that she was unable even to like him, and stating that he 'had a wall around him.' She suspected sex play with his foster sister.

A psychiatric assessment at this time suggested that foster placement was problematic. As a result, Jamie was placed in a treatment centre for older boys when he was 10 years old. His initial fear and loneliness gradually lessened, and six months later his case worker indicated that he was making progress in getting along with other boys and was showing fewer 'feminine' characteristics. For the next two years, no information was recorded. By this time, Jamie's case worker believed he was ready for a group home: 'He had progressed in ego strength, self-assertion and in his male identification. He seemed to be overcoming his irrational fears and was handling community activities quite well. He had made good progress in school and was in Grade 7 at the age of 13 years.'

The transfer to a group home took place smoothly. Still, Jamie seemed to be somewhat defensive and manipulative, but he endured the change with a 'more intellectual approach' than before. In this home, he was able to be in the middle position with two strong parental figures. Jamie made progress in this home over the next two years and was visited weekly by his Children's Aid worker. He was described as very insecure, but having a sense of fun and spontaneity. He still had difficulty in trusting his foster parents and other boys, but he did make a couple of friends. By 15 years of age, enrolled in the first year of a commercial course at a nearby collegiate institute, he was having much difficulty and wondered whether he would continue.

Unfortunately, his group home was closed because of the foster mother's illness, and Jamie, along with some other boys, was forced to move to another group home. Jamie was angry and upset about the move, and again became demanding and aggravating. His fears and anxieties were dealt with sensitively by his case worker, and he gradually adjusted. Camp experiences were enjoyed, and Jamie hoped to become a junior counsellor the next season.

By his seventeenth year, Jamie was doing better in school. In the group home, he was still described as effeminate, relating better and more easily to adults than to his peers. He was often resented by his peers because of his attempts to please and impress the adults. He did, however, take on a leadership role in the home, being several years older than the other boys. He still needed a great deal of individual attention, which his group home parents attempted to give him.

As he approached the age of majority, his case worker helped him plan for the future. Jamie leaned heavily on his worker and foster parents, at one point requesting that they adopt him. In preparation for his discharge from the agency he was moved to a half-way house, where he was described as dependent, immature, and childishly irritating. He barked like a dog and at times yelled and screamed. He was fortunate to be supported by a case worker who gave him consistent guidance in the planning of his discharge. He gained financial assistance to complete his course in community college. During this time, he worked nights at a children's residence. The final description of Jamie, on his discharge from care, stated that he appeared very vulnerable despite his ability to have found a way of supporting himself. It was noted that he had difficulty trusting anyone, was often depressed, had no real friends, had a poor self-image, and was fearful of meeting the expectations of the world. He was aware of his inability to form lasting relationships, but refused an opportunity to pursue therapy to help him resolve these difficulties.

Jamie was a child on whom there was relatively extensive information. His prolonged institutional care until six and one-half years of age occurred during and after the rehabilitation program in the Neil McNeil home. Hence, considerable attention was given to enhance his emotional well-being. Latterly, he had the good luck to find professional workers and caregivers who gave sensitive support to his needs. However, committed, long-term attachment was never possible. Although he progressed intellectually, his emotional and social growth were thwarted. One wonders whether Jamie had any sense of himself outside the framework of the Children's Aid agency. Was the agency his surrogate parent? What potential would he have for an enduring mature dependency with another person? What inner resources and external support had helped him achieve apparent stability, with residual good feelings about the agency?

June

June had only four placements, the last with a caring foster family. She was admitted to the institution when she was nine and one-half months of age. Several siblings were also placed with the agency as the result of family breakdown. After six months, June was placed with a foster family, but was returned to the agency five months later. Prior to her final foster placement, June spent six months in another institution. Throughout all those moves June was reported to be a rather placid, good-natured child. This fourth placement proved to be an excellent choice for her, and she was happily accepted by this family. Adoption was discussed, but the family felt they could not afford this, for there were several other children in the home – three sons and an infant. June remained here from her fourth year and grew up in this family. Soon after her foster family took June into their care, they moved from the province, and June accompanied them. Thus, communication and case notes were minimal; another agency now provided supervision.

June's progress in this family indicated a secure, adequately func-tioning young person. When she was 12 years old, a request from one of her biological sisters for contact with June was denied on the basis that the sister's emotionally disturbed behaviour might affect June ad-versely. A report at this time indicated that June was an attractive, friendly girl with a healthy attitude toward school and good peer rela-tionships. By age 16, she had won a trophy as the best athlete in her year. She had a steady boyfriend and planned to complete Grade 12. The foster family were happy with her and were prepared to give her a home 'for many years to come.'

When June reached the age of majority (18), she and her biological sisters met at the agency to receive background information on their family. They expressed delight at meeting one another. One last brief notation soon after indicated that June was fully employed and living independently of her foster family, although maintaining contact with them. June's story, although filled with time gaps in recording, is heart-warming. There was continuity in her care, apparent warmth and attach-ment, acceptance of family values, and adequate records. Her capacity to develop mature dependencies and independence had apparently emerged unscathed. What prompted her to seek out her biological sisters and information about her parents is unclear, but this is not an uncommon pattern for wards of Children's Aid.

Evaluation of the Contrast Group

As indicated earlier in this chapter, it was difficult to evaluate the men-tal health of this group of 14 children at the time of their discharge, or to anticipate their future, based on their records. However, we at-tempted to classify them according to *good, poor,* or *uncertain* outcomes. Four of the young people were then judged to have good prospects. Five appeared to have uncertain futures, and the remaining five were seen as having poor prospects.

Although these children had not had any consistent evaluation on the measures used for our original study group, an attempt was made to evaluate their well-being in respect to one fundamental aspect of security theory – the ability to form significant relationships with adults – and to look at the involvement of significant people in their lives.

Significant Relationships

The degree to which these subjects had achieved mature dependencies along with the ability to act independently became clearer when their records were examined in detail. One significant factor in the histories of those children who achieved both these states was a significant relationship with an understanding adult. Four of the 14 children enjoyed this advantage with their caregivers. They were treated with sensitivity and respect, and were warmly accepted into family life. These four were the children who appeared to have a good prospect for success in later life.

One of the four was June, who was discussed in this chapter. Another positive story is about Rose. She was a premature infant who spent her first 10 weeks in hospital and the following four and one-half years in an institution. Then, she was placed in a foster home, where she remained for 13 years. When she reached the age of majority, Rose's foster parents offered her a permanent home, and she was still living with them at age 21. An added positive factor for Rose was the long-term (eight and one-half years) involvement of her social worker. She also received excellent care from her foster parents. Rose passed through stages of immature dependent security and by her early adolescence was described as strong-willed, hyperactive, and having poor social skills. Her foster parents tolerated these problems and continued to provide direction, support, and affection. At the age of majority, Rose was working part-time and attending vocational school, and was demonstrating maturity and independence.

A third child in this group was David, who spent his first six years in institutional settings, demonstrating considerable developmental delay. He was chosen for fostering by a couple who had known him in his last institution. This couple were clearly committed to him and appeared to cherish him. There were many problems as David grew, but by 13 years David was reported to be functioning intellectually in the bright-normal range, with some perceptual problems. He was frequently seen as insecure and felt threatened if he made mistakes. His foster parents dealt with him competently and with understanding. For example, several episodes of disrespect and hostility toward his foster mother prompted her to call a family meeting. David was confronted, and his father told him that if he did not want to meet the family's expectations, he could return to the institution. The other children (all natural children of the foster parents) protested against their father's position, saying they wanted David to stay. David was deeply moved by their caring for him. This resulted in a dramatic change in his behaviour. When he was 16 years old, he was adopted by these caring and sensitive parents.

The fourth member of this group who seemed to have potential for success was Albert. He had experienced nine placements before he was discharged at age 21. Admitted to care from hospital at 10 weeks of age owing to his mother's inability to care for him, he had experienced seven different placements by the age of 11 years. These included five institutional settings and two adoption-probation breakdowns. He was then placed in an agency group home, where he remained for five years. He was seen as an anxious young person, striving for acceptance but vulnerable to criticism; he could be explosive and aggressive if he felt rejected. However, he made some progress, over this period through the assistance of the competent staff. Then an experienced mental health professional and his wife offered their home as a placement for Albert. He remained with them for the next year and a half.

Albert appeared to be comfortable in this family and showed increasing maturity and confidence. However, he shied away from their expectation of closer emotional attachment. His foster parents offered to adopt him, but Albert did not welcome this. However, the assistance and sensitivity that he received in this home helped him to make considerable progress. His immature dependencies diminished, and he appeared to be showing a capacity for mature dependency. Yet, when faced with the offer of adoption, it seemed that his anxieties and immaturities overwhelmed him. Did he fear another failure? At the age of 17, Albert decided to move from his foster home into a private boarding establishment. In that setting, he maintained contact with his foster parents, and became self-supporting. He made many friends for whom, surprisingly, he became a source of advice and support. When he was discharged from care at age 21, he was functioning well in the community and at times was in touch with his foster parents.

Foster Fathers

Another significant factor that emerged from evaluating these records was the role of the foster father. Five children were judged to have poor prospects for healthy maturation. Of these, three (all male) were reported to have had poor relationships with their foster fathers, who were either uninvolved, passive and indifferent to the ward, or at times openly hostile. In the fourth case, the foster mother was a widow, and there was no adult male in the home. In the fifth case, the foster mother died when the boy was 11 years old; the family was under much stress and fell apart. When the foster child was in his teens and the natural son a few years older, the father abandoned them, leaving them to care for themselves. At age 17, the foster child was charged with theft and jailed. Unfortunately, there is no further record of him.

Another child, Louis, whose prognosis had been categorized as uncertain, had nine placements and 15 case workers. His last placement, a foster home in which he lived for seven years, was considered a sound placement, but it is clear from the case notes that his foster mother was a domineering person, strong-willed, and unskilled in managing a child with so many needs. The foster father was minimally involved, and Louis regarded him with hostility. The boy began to demonstrate 'feminine' characteristics and sought approval in many inappropriate ways. Psychiatric and psychological assessments recommended treatment for him and counselling for his foster parents, which they refused. After nine years in this home, Louis was placed in an agency group home. Here he received professional help but was slow to respond. He was seen as having low self-esteem, much underlying anger, and uncertainty about himself. By age 15, he was acting out, stealing and sometimes absenting himself from the home. At 18 years, he refused to commit himself to a therapeutic program, and no extension of wardship was sought. At this time he was seen as unreliable, but with some capabilities. On discharge, he appeared to have no significant male or female relationships that might lead to mature dependence.

A number of these young people had a record of conflict with the law. In five cases, each boy was charged with theft. One of the wards was discharged from Children's Aid care to a training school when he was 15 years old. Of these five cases, four had either a poor relationship or no relationship with their long-term foster father. The fifth, who lived with the widow, had no male role model in his life.

In contrast, of the four children whose prospects appeared to be good, three had excellent relationships with their foster fathers in their long-term placements. The fathers were regarded as involved, caring, positive role models. Within the group categorized as uncertain were some children who appeared damaged by their institutional care and short-term placements, yet who in their teens were fortunate enough to find highly competent foster fathers and male group home workers. Such men seemed able to establish supportive and consistent relationships, to the benefit of these vulnerable young people.

The foregoing observations cannot be considered statistically significant, but the consistency that has been noted should not be ignored. The father's role may be highly significant in the development of vulnerable young people. Further, it has become increasingly evident that the quality of family life affects the broader quality of life in our society. The importance to foster children of a healthy, well functioning family, with positive parent role models, cannot be ignored.

Historical Perspective

This small study, carried out with the cooperation of the Catholic Children's Aid Society of Metropolitan Toronto, focused on a group of children in care from 1956–74. It sought to discover what happened to these children, and revealed some of the unfortunate discontinuities in their lives. It also revealed some of the problems faced by agencies charged with the care of children whose biological families cannot carry out their parenting role. What this study could not address is the specific reasons for these discontinuities, which clearly did not serve the best interests of these children.

During the period of these children's placements, variable public funding from year to year created external pressures, and internal agency functions fluctuated according to numbers of case workers and particular needs of clients. The sheer size of the demand for foster care led to much pressure upon case workers and, at times, many changes in assignments and caseloads. This resulted in breakdowns in communication, and even misunderstandings about the needs of the child. Career changes for case workers often led to service disruption and a breakdown of trust for the child, and probably for the foster parents as well. New case workers needed time to review records and to become familiar with their clients. Crises in the families and the burden of heavy caseloads put much pressure on the worker. Supervisors and case workers were constantly aware of the tenuous hold they had on the allegiance of the foster family. In addition, the child's relationship with the biological family was often in chaos or broken down. The discontinuities in these children's lives were ongoing and related to agency conditions as well as their natural families, and often could not be overcome.

The conditions described here occurred in the 1960s and '70s. In the last two decades, attempts to provide more effective service to children have brought about changes in the management of all Children's Aid Societies. Legislative changes have strongly supported assistance to families in trouble. The current focus is on non-intrusive techniques and a commitment to involve natural families in all planning and decisions affecting their children. In most situations, involvement means their actual presence and participation in these discussions. Every attempt is made to provide ongoing support and assistance. Language and cultural differences are now acknowledged in the participation of multilingual case workers. Such measures attempt to address the importance of early attachment and a child's roots in the natural family. Every effort is made to avoid the admission of children to agency care. Emergency situations and cases of sexual, physical, or extreme emotional abuse are the exception. As well, foster parents now experience much more intense professional preparation for their role. They take part in orientation sessions and opportunities for discussion with experienced foster parents and case workers before they receive a child into their home. The expectation is that they will accept visits of the natural family to their home, and will help the child maintain a relationship with the natural family.

Summary

This small study illuminates the impact of the service system on the lives of children. Four of this group of 14 subjects appeared to be functioning in a way that could be regarded to predict successful adaptation. Another five appeared unstable and lacking healthy assets at the age of discharge. Three of these subjects had already experienced periods of time in training school or in jail for theft. The remaining five appeared to have a poor self-image on discharge, and prospects for the future seemed poor. These five children, although experiencing a relatively small number of foster homes (five through nine), each had more case workers in their lives than foster placements. Each had emotional problems in the growing years. Their future adaptation seemed a matter of uncertainty.

Keeping in mind the meagreness of our data on this contrast group, clearly demonstrable outcomes are elusive. Nevertheless, one clear conclusion is the fact that discontinuities of homes and caretakers over their growing years was the norm for these children. Not only was their caretaking experience vastly different from that of children reared in their own families; it also differs from the experience of the children of our long-term study. The second obvious factor is the absence of a case worker with a long-term caring commitment to these children's welfare (as shown in Table 10). The third fact to emerge from individual records is the diminished quality of life of two-thirds of this group when compared with those of our first study. And finally, some children experienced sufficient healthy support along their journey to maturity to have gained confidence and skills that prepared them for the tasks of adulthood.

Only constant vigilance will keep agencies alert to the impact of any policy, no matter how well intentioned, on its children. Systems are imperfect, and some children will inevitability be the victims of neglect. There are children, left in disorganized and ineffective families, who will become increasingly marginalized despite the efforts of case workers who attempt to keep a family intact. Social workers themselves vary in capabilities, knowledge, and dedication. Further, funding is limited, and decisions affecting the best interests of a child are made with social, emotional, and monetary considerations in counterbalance. The commitment of Children's Aid Societies is to protect the essentially helpless children in their care, who have no reliable, caring person dedicated to their journey to maturity. The task is awesome. The question remains, how best to carry it out.

11

In Retrospect

As we evaluate the huge amount of data gathered over 30 years and consider the direction of events in the lives of our experimental group of subjects, we recognize that we have gained insights not only into their lives, but have also heightened our understanding of human development.

Our team was impressed by the value of consistency in the lives of growing children as a basis of providing a secure foothold for development. This conclusion was constantly underlined. From infancy, when the presence of a consistent maternal figure secures a child's trust, and throughout childhood, when reliable standards and values establish guidelines for future behaviour, consistency provides the security for a child's healthy functioning. The fact that the research team shared a similar knowledge base in child development as well as a confidence in the conceptual framework of security theory facilitated their cooperative effort to initiate a therapy program, in the collection and analysis of data, and in the support of the case worker's application of theory to practice. Her interpretation of children's behaviour to parents, and her recommendations of sound parenting practices, sprang from a consistent frame of reference that seemed to strengthen many families' capacity to implement them. Hence, confidence was established for case worker, parents, and children alike.

Those children whose adoptive parents provided consistent, reliable rules of behaviour stabilized and moved on more successfully in their development than did those who were exposed to inconsistent parenting. It became evident that a child's healthy sense of self within the family depended on the reliability of a system of values expressed in parenting practices. As a child increasingly identified with the adoptive family, he or she exuded a blossoming sense of self that was based on trust in the family and in the world. Evidence of the strength of this identification can be seen in such children as George and Maurice (Chapter 3), whose developmental pathways differed radically but both of whom strongly identified with their families. Both families initially relied heavily on the systematic input of the case worker, whose detailed, practical recommendations provided guidelines that supported the children's development in the family and in the community.

One of the remarkable aspects of this 30-year study was the presence of the same case worker throughout. Her identification with the future well-being of the children started when she was responsible for implementing the therapeutic program in the institution. She participated in the decisions about the children's placements in families and, when the institution closed, took on the multiple roles of research data collector, advocate for the children, and case worker for the subjects and their families. Such long-term devotion undoubtedly contributed to the overall successful adaptation of these children through their adolescent years. The role of a caring person in the lives of 'at risk' children has now been demonstrated both clinically and by research.[1]

Few studies have had the opportunity to trace the role of a case worker so exhaustively, with all its successes, disappointments, mistakes, and emotional attachments, over time. A steady source of strength for our case worker was the presence of the research team to assist her with agonizing compromises in the children's lives, with planning the best resolution for unexpected events, with strategies to remove obstacles in the family's dealing with a child, and with facilitating the child's progress in school. Without such support, her long-term commitment might not have succeeded. The need for supervision of any professional working with families has long been recognized by social agencies, which have established structures to support this. One of the regrettable facts faced by child care agencies is the discontinuity of service to children and their families. Case workers may change roles within agencies, move from one agency to another, pick up new caseloads, begin to serve children and families and change jobs yet again before they are able to become acquainted with their clients. Such discontinuity has repercussions on the worker–supervisor rela-

---

1 Werner, E.E. (1985). Stress and protective factors in children's lives. In A.R. Nichol (Ed.), *Longitudinal studies in child psychology and psychiatry.* Chichester, U.K.: John Wiley & Sons.

tionship, further diluting the quality of service. Added to this fact is the burden of heavy caseloads. These result in remote, impersonal service: children and families may never become 'persons' to their case workers. The data collected on our second study, of a contrast group of children who were under the traditional care of the agency, clearly demonstrated such discontinuity. The most extreme example was the child who experienced 21 changes of home and 21 changes of case workers on his road to maturity.

The opportunity to work with our subjects while they were infants in the institution deepened our understanding of the environmental and social requirements for normal human development. When we first observed these children in their sterile environment, we projected on them expectations for 'normal,' age-related behaviours. Further, we were aware that attempts to place these children in homes usually ended in failure. Simultaneously, we were in the midst of the first swell of interest in the impact on infants of 'maternal deprivation.' Therefore, we assumed on first contact with the children that they were emotionally disturbed. Many months of experience, however, led us to question our original assumptions. As we observed the slow emergence of relatively normal (albeit immature) developmental behaviours, we recognized that many of the children's bizarre behaviours were the result of lack of development. Not only were these children maternally deprived, but they lacked the normal stimulation usually provided by loving and attentive caretakers. (At this time we had not the benefit of Bronfenbrenner's (1968) monumental survey of early deprivation in mammals[2] which had not yet been published.) Furthermore, the lack of differentiation between the children's life in cribs and their life outside cribs precluded recognition of the significance of flow of time, which is an integral part of life in a normal home. Night and day were indistinguishable to these children. The course of a day was largely spent in cribs, and was marked by three separate meals, a sponge bath, sporadic clothing changes, and (after 30 months of age) a limited play period. Thus, the children were unable to grasp such concepts as 'before' and 'after.' We began to understand that maternal deprivation and stimulus deprivation were inextricably entwined, and that the lack of normal daily activity in the lives of these children precluded their

2 Bronfenbrenner, U. (1968). Early deprivation in mammals: A cross-species analysis. In G. Newton & S. Levine (eds.), *Early experience and behaviour.* Springfield, IL: C.C. Thomas.

behaving in ways that were expected of children reared in homes. Hence, we were not treating emotionally disturbed children, but rather were initiating them into a 'normal' stream of environmental events and expectations. The problem was not to 'undo' emotional disturbance but to generate emotional energy by affectionate interactions, and to provide environmental supports to channel that energy into appropriate activities.

One of our astonishing discoveries was that the children did not spontaneously play when given an opportunity. The arousal of interest in toys and in other children as playmates proved difficult. Months elapsed before play was evident. As well, monumental staff input was required to create interest in most normal activities, such as dressing, bathing, and eating. The experience of satisfaction from efforts toward helping themselves eluded these children for months.

At the same time, we were puzzled by a paradoxically subtle aspect of the children's behaviour as revealed by the Flint Infant Security Scale. In the beginning of our study, when each infant's environment seemed equally sterile and uneventful, each child demonstrated an unexpected drop in security score. This was associated with a change from one seemingly identical crib and room to another. The implication was that the children must have been aware of subtle differences that demanded their adaptation to a strange situation. What created this insecurity?

As we pondered this question, we concluded that the phenomenon might be associated with definition of self. We came to realize that not only children but adults living in a restricted environment rely on the constancy of minute aspects of their surroundings to maintain their sense of security. Hence, in the lives of these deprived infants, many sensory experiences defined their sense of self: a lump in the mattress of their crib, peeled paint on the wall of their cubicle, the shadow cast by the sun at a particular time of day, the sound of a familiar footstep, the noise of a child rocking his crib in the next cubicle, a light bulb in the ceiling. Hence, change of almost imperceptible degree to caretakers was anxiety provoking for these children because it posed a threat to their stable world, around which they had defined themselves. The same reaction to change has been observed in older adults, particularly those in institutions, who are no longer able to take control of their lives. Even minor changes can provoke seemingly exaggerated anxiety.

One of the surprising aspects of our initial contact with the institutionalized children was the caretakers' apparent obliviousness to the environmental assets that create conditions for normal human development. Yet, they believed they were carrying out their jobs satisfactorily. They were not 'bad' people, but rather people whose focus was on other dimensions of living than child rearing. The administrators, who had to staff the institution 24 hours a day, naturally were concerned to maintain as happy a staff as possible. The fact that a large number of the caretakers were nuns in residence precluded the need to consider traditional eight-hour shifts to supervise the children. However, it heightened the necessity to focus more on the needs of the caretakers than on the children. Hence, the routine of the institution functioned around appropriate times for adults to have meals, go to chapel, do the laundry, take rest breaks, and provide care. The children were rarely thought of as individuals, but rather were managed in groups according to chronological age. Such a practice discouraged the recognition of each child as a unique person. The resulting cycle of action and reaction caused increased depression and withdrawal in the children. The longer they remained in the institution, the more apathetic and unresponsive they became.

When the rehabilitation program began, the administrative problems of staffing eight-hour shifts with many new caretakers was exacerbated by the unrewarding behaviours of the children. A training program in child development was initiated to inform and encourage new staff to focus on the needs of the children and to feel satisfaction for the emerging (albeit minuscule) steps forward in each child's development. Particular emphasis was placed on the importance of providing a foundation of trust through a relationship with staff. Only unrelenting focus on the needs of the children prevented staff from succumbing once more to allowing their own comfort to take precedence over that of the children. In retrospect, we realized that any system of institutional care, whether for children, elderly persons, or those who are chronically ill and relatively helpless, lends itself to the same urgent demands from staff who seek some satisfaction for maintaining their workload.

One of the first revelations of this study was that the depriving institutional environment affected the children in vastly different ways. This difference was notable even by nine months of age. Assessing the infants' mental health on the Flint Infant Security Scale revealed astonishing variation among children whose stay in the institution was identical in terms of length, type of experience, and caretaking personnel. Examination of physical status and social history revealed no differences that seemed significant. These individual differences in security scores were evident by four months of age, and by nine months of age were displayed in an astounding difference of 43 points for two infants (+.40 vs. –.03). This represented the difference between infants showing a normal pattern of mental health (+.40) and infants who were seriously 'at risk' (–.03).

Such unexpected differences encouraged us to proceed with the environmental changes in the belief that at least some of the children could recover from their early deprivation.[3] As the therapeutic milieu began to affect the children, each continued to respond individually. In an attempt to evaluate what assets in a child's make-up contributed to his or her emerging mental health, we examined both security scores and staff daily reports. We identified three dimensions of personality and response, one or another of which seemed to predominate in each child.

Some children were socially oriented and responded most directly to physical contact and personal interactions. These children also responded most quickly to intervention. Other children were interested in interaction only after they had learned to engage with play materials, which could then be used as a vehicle for personal interactions with them. These children took longer to 'reach' and to respond to the therapeutic milieu. A third (and smaller) group of children maintained a distance from both direct personal contact and active interest in play materials. These children were the cautious 'watchers' and were the most resistant to the change in environment. Staff had to await their willingness to respond as they gradually allowed themselves to be drawn into the events around them.

On examination of our security profiles of our subjects as adults, these characteristics seemed to have been modified by the events of their lives. However, their histories suggested a consistent approach to life that originated in infancy and early childhood. Recognizing that individuals are too complex to lend themselves to clearly defined classification, we made use of the idea of three different orientations to their approach to life's tasks. We discovered, as general characterizations of an individual's basic approach to life's events, they were useful means to initiate intervention.

3 Flint, B.M. (1959). *The security of infants.* Toronto: University of Toronto Press.

One awareness that has emerged from our long-term study is the degree to which early severe deprivation can be relieved. When this study began (1956), the consensus was that recovery from early deprivation was questionable. It has since been demonstrated that such an outlook was unduly pessimistic. There are many survivors. What then, has this study contributed to our understanding of them?

The duration of our study permitted us to explore the process of recovery, and has demonstrated the length of time required to achieve a state of emotional well-being and a comfortable sense of self. The analysis of our Rorschach data demonstrated that eight of the 10 subjects had achieved normal patterns of thought by 15 years of age. However, their profiles were 'immature,' more closely resembling those of 12-year-olds. The fact that these children had taken so long to acquire mainstream patterns of conceptualization was a revelation, and provided reassurance that the benign impact of long-term adoptive or foster care was salutary. Related to this issue was the optimal age for placement in a home in order for the child to benefit. It was reassuring to find that one of our most satisfactorily functioning subjects, George (Chapter 3), was placed in his adoptive home after four years of age. He identified well with his adoptive family, and was happily emancipated from it, retaining a good relationship with his parents and sister. As an adult, he was functioning at a high level in his job and community, and was happily married. Jane (Chapter 3) was placed at four years, seven months of age; she too adapted well to her foster family, assuming their name on her own initiative on reaching maturity. Certainly, individual differences are powerful factors for success, and it is risky to generalize from a few cases. Nevertheless, we are impressed that placement even after four years of age does not preclude identification with non-biological families.

The histories of our subjects suggest that most of them have made a much healthier adaptation in all life areas than would have been anticipated, considering their degree of early deprivation. We based this conclusion on evaluation of their peer relationships, self-esteem, careers and hobbies, family relationships, attitudes to physical health, and their religion or general philosophy of life.

World unrest, war, famine, and transient families have created in the 1990s a need to care for hordes of homeless children. Institutionalization seems inevitable for many of them. The authors still cling to the model that family life provides the best milieu for child rearing. Yet, many children will never find a family, even as foster or adoptive children. Economic constraints in a worldwide depressed economy threaten the implementation of many aspects of institutional care that we now know can maintain at least minimal health. It is possible to provide humane child rearing in an institutional setting, but only the constant vigilance of knowledgeable and caring adults will create a nurturing environment that will provide a climate for normal development. Trusting relationships and provision of opportunities for children to explore and act on their environment are the foundations for any adequate child-rearing milieu. Institutional life, and even day care programs, can be enriched by the application of knowledge arising from such experiences as ours.

APPENDIX 1
Phase III Interview Format

The following interview was conducted as a follow-up with each of 20 subjects from the 85 studied in phase I.

Family
1. How often do you see your parents?
2. Do you drop in or wait to be invited?
3. Do you feel obligated to see them regularly?
4. Do you wish you could see them more often?
5. Do you ever ask their advice?   Mother
                                      Father

If no, why?

If yes:
6. For what kinds of things? e.g., mortgage, job, child care, clothes, personal finances, shopping, friends?
7. Do you take their advice?
8. Would you be uneasy if you couldn't get their opinion about a decision?
9. What do you enjoy doing with your parents?
10. What do your parents do that annoys you?
11. Do they sometimes hurt your feelings?
12. How do you react?
13. Would you like to be on better terms with your parents?
14. Do you feel your parents interfere in your life?
15. Would you make a decision if you knew your parents disapproved?
16. Would you   • worry about this?
                   • resent this?

Spouse
1. How often do you see in-laws?   Mother
                                        Father
2. How would you describe your relationship with them?   Mother
                                                             Father
3. What kinds of things do you and your mate like to do together?
4. What kinds of things do you do separately?
5. Who does the   dishes?
                  cooking?
                  cleaning?
                  laundry?
6. What do you feel is the most important thing you do with your child? e.g., prepare good food, keep clean, give affection, play, get good babysitters, have fun together.
7. What does your spouse think is the most important thing she does with your child?
8. When do you all enjoy each other best?
9. If you both work, what are your babysitting arrangements?
10. Do you often disagree about the way to handle the baby's behaviour? How do you settle this?
11. What do you like best about your mate?
12. What does she do that annoys you?
13. How do you let him/her know you are annoyed?
14. What do you do that annoys him/her?
15. How does she let you know?
16. Do you try not to do it again?

Peers
1. Do you see your brothers and sisters very often?
2. Do you have a favourite on whom you rely for help and advice? e.g., children, cooking, money.
3. Who are your closest friends?
4. What do you do together? e.g., holidays, movies, etc.
5. Do you ask their advice? e.g., on clothes, child rearing, money matters, lifestyles.

Vocation
1. Do you have a job now?
2. Have you ever been out of a job?
3. How did you feel?

4. How did you manage financially?
5. Do you feel you are paid well enough for the work you do?
6. What made you choose this kind of job?
7. Do you like your job?
8. What do you like best about it?
9. Are you good at it?
10. Would you prefer to find a different job? Where?
11. What kind of job would you like to have if you could change?
12. What kinds of jobs have you had in the 13 years since we last contacted you?
13. What was the best?

Avocation
1. What do you do for fun?
     Sports
     Hobbies
     Interests
     TV
     Reading
2. Do these cost you a lot of money? Time?
3. What are you best at?
4. What do you have the most fun at?
5. Do you belong to any clubs?
6. What do you like best to do on a Saturday night?
     Movie
     Sport
     Stay home
     Go dancing
     Be with friends
     Be alone

Philosophy: Religion
1. Do you go to church? What church?
2. How often?
3. With whom?
4. Are you involved in church activities?
5. Do you plan to take your children to church?
6. Are you concerned about their religious training?
7. Are you as religious as your parents?
8. How have your religious beliefs changed?

9. Do you discuss this with your parents?
10. Do your religious beliefs help you in your daily living?
11. Do you believe that there is a just god who does look after people?
12. How then do you explain 'when bad things happen to good people'?
13. Do you feel that you could cope with almost any tragedy that you might have to face?
14. What would be the worst thing that could happen to you?
15. How would you react to it?
16. Are your plans for the future hampered by the threat of nuclear war?

Philosophy: Self
1. Are you usually on time for work?
        doctor's appointments?
        dates?
2. If you felt overcharged for merchandise or repairs (e.g, car) would you complain?
3. Would you help a friend to get a square deal?
4. Do you like to be by yourself? Why?
5. Would you go to a movie or hockey game by yourself?
6. Do you enjoy meeting new people?
7. If invited to a party with people you did not know well what would you do? Go? Make an excuse? Stay home?
8. Do you ask others' advice about buying clothes?
9. Do you consider yourself a smart dresser?
10. Would it upset you to miss a meal? Breakfast? Lunch?
11. What steps do you take to keep healthy? e.g., eating, sleeping, visiting doctor, keeping clean, vitamins, laxatives.

Philosophy: Money
1. Do you feel you have enough money for your needs?
2. Are you paying board, renting, supporting self?
3. Are you a good money manager?
4. What do you need that you cannot afford?
5. Do you feel elated when you get a bargain?
6. How often does your money run out?
7. What do you do then?
8. Do you use credit cards?
9. Why?

10. Have you ever been on Unemployment Insurance? Welfare?
11. What would you do if you won a million dollars in a lottery?
12. Do you every buy new clothes on impulse? Other articles?
13. Do you currently have: a mortgage, unpaid bill for car, TV, appliances?
14. Do these worry you?

Emotions
 1. What parts of your life do you most enjoy?
 2. Do you like new things?
 3. How do you feel about changes in your life? e.g., moving, job, marriage.
 4. What do you most fear – spiders, snakes, mice, crowds?
 5. How you do act when you are frightened?
 6. What do you worry about?
 7. How do you act when you are worried?
 8. What kinds of things make you angry?
 9. What do you do about it?
10. Do you have a temper?
11. Does it get you in trouble?
12. Are you generally happy?
13. What kinds of things make you happy?
14. Are you very sensitive to criticism?
15. How often do you get discouraged?
16. What discourages you?
17. What do you do when you are discouraged? e.g., try again, talk to friends, eat, give up, spend money, talk to parents, smoke, drink?

APPENDIX 2
Phase II Follow-up Questionnaire

This questionnaire was given to 28 adoptive and foster families as a follow-up assessment of the case worker's role in the adoptive process.

Questions
1. How would you describe the role [the case worker] has played in your life?
   - at the time your child was placed in your home
   - after your child's initial adjustment to your family
   - over the elementary school years
   - at present.
2. What are the most helpful things [the case worker] has done for your family?
3. What are the least helpful things she has done?

Responses
Examination of the answers led to an analysis of the most often-repeated themes in the parents' responses. These were categorized under three headings: attitude of the case worker, types of involvement, and intensity and duration.

Attitude of the Worker
- Interest in children – friend to children, does things for them
- interest in parents
- Interest in other members of the family
- Friendly and enjoys talking; is frank, considerate, kind, reassuring, understanding, tactful, encouraging,

- shows good judgment
- Listens graciously; parents have confidence in her; is sincere, warm, dedicated

Types of Involvement
- Counsels parents re: background of child
- Offers suggestions – specific troubleshooting
- Teaches, suggests methods of parenting
- Offers insights into children's problems
- Prods families to action
- Supports
- Discusses
- Acts as mediator with school; helps teacher as well as parents
- Provides referrals for professional help: psychologist, mental health clinic, hospital, boys' village
- Anticipates problem; prepares parents
- Watches out for the children
- Offers material re: child rearing – literature, movies, lectures
- Builds parents' self-confidence
- Offers friendship

Intensity and Duration
- Back-up if needed
- Large role in family (e.g., one parent would not have kept child without her support)
- Selects children challenging to parents
- Always there if needed – frequent recourse
- 'Dear friend' of the family
- Sustained contact (11 years); readily available by telephone; often initiates contact; frequent, regular visits
- Record keeping gives parents an idea of progress (may be threatening to some parents).

Bibliography

Ackerman, N. (Ed.). (1967). *Expanding theory and practices in family therapy.* New York: Family Service Association of America.

Ainsworth, M.D. (1962). The effects of maternal deprivation: A review of findings and controversy in the context of research strategy. In *Deprivation of maternal care: A reassessment of its effects.* Geneva: World Health Organization.

Ainsworth, M.D. (1963). The development of infant–mother interaction among the Ganda. In B.M. Foss (Ed.), *Determinants of infant behaviour* (vol. 2). London: Methuen.

Ainsworth, M.D. (1964). Patterns of attachment behaviour shown by the infant in interaction with his mother. *Merrill–Palmer Quarterly, 10,* 51.

Ainsworth, M.D. (1969). Object relations, dependency and attachment: A theoretical review of the infant–mother relationship. *Child Development, 40,* 969–1025.

Ainsworth, M.D. (1972). Development of infant–mother attachment. In B.M. Caldwell & H.N. Reccuiti (Eds.), *Child development research* (vol. 3). Chicago: University of Chicago Press.

Ainsworth, M.D. (1974). Infant–mother attachment and social development: Socialization as a product of responsiveness to signals. In M. Richards (Ed.), *The integration of the child into the social world.* New York & Cambridge: Cambridge University Press.

Ainsworth, M.D. (1982). Attachment, retrospect and prospect. In C.M. Parkes & H. Stevenson (Eds.), *The place of attachment in human behavior.* New York: Basic Books.

Ainsworth, M.D. (1984). The development of mother–infant attachment. In J. Belsky (Ed.), *In the beginning.* New York: Columbia University Press.

Ainsworth, M.D., & Bell, S.M. (1969). Some contemporary patterns of mother – infant interaction in the feeding situation. In A. Ambrose (Ed.), *Stimulation in early infancy*. New York: Academic Press.

Ainsworth, M.D., & Wittig, B.A. (1969). Attachment and exploratory behaviour of one-year-olds in a strange situation. In B.M. Foss (Ed.), *Determinants of infant behaviour* (vol. 4). London: Methuen.

Ambrose, J.A. (1961a). The concept of a critical period for the development of social responsiveness. In B.M. Foss (Ed.), *Determinants of infant behaviour* (vol. 2.). London: Methuen.

Ambrose, J.A. (1961b). Development of the sibling response in early infancy. In B.M. Foss (Ed.), *Determinants of infant behaviour* (vol. 1). London: Methuen.

Ames, L.B., Metraux, R.W., & Walker, R.N. (1971). *Adolescent Rorschach responses*. New York: Brunner/Mazel.

Anastasi, A. (1968). *Psychological testing*. New York: Macmillan.

Bakwin, H. (1949). Emotional deprivation in infants. *Journal of Pediatrics, 35*, 512–21.

Bayley, N. (1965, July). *Research in child development: A longitudinal perspective. Merrill – Palmer Quarterly, 2* (3), 183–208.

Beardslee, W.R. (1989, April). The role of self-understanding in resilient individuals. *American Journal of Orthopsychiatry, 59* (2), 266–278.

Bender, L. (1947). Psychopathic behaviour disorders in children. In R.M. Linder & R.V. Seliger (Eds.), *Handbook of correctional psychology*. New York: Philosophical Library.

Beres, D., & Obers, S. (1950). The effects of extreme deprivation in infancy on psychic structure in adolescence. *Psychoanalytical Study of Childhood, 5*, 121–40.

Blishen, B.R. (1958, November). The construction and use of an occupational class scale. *Canadian Journal of Economic and Political Science, 24*, 519–31.

Bloom-Feshbach, J., Bloom-Feshbach, S., & Associates (Eds.). (1987). *The psychology of separation and loss*. San Francisco: Jossey-Bass.

Bortner, M., & Birch, H.G. (1969). Patterns of intellectual ability in emotionally disturbed and brain-damaged children. *Journal Special Education, 3* (4), 351–69.

Bowlby, J. (1951). *Maternal care and mental health*. Geneva: World Health Organization.

Bowlby, J. (1958). The nature of the child's tie to his mother. International Journal of Psychoanalysis, *39*, 350–73.

Bowlby, J. (1962). Childhood bereavement and psychiatric illness. In

D. Richter, J.M. Tanner, & L. Taylor, & O.L. Zangwill (Eds.), *Aspects of psychiatric research*. London: Oxford University Press.

Bowlby, J. (1969). *Attachment and loss* (vol. 1: Attachment). London: Hogarth Press.

Bowlby, J. (1973). *Attachment and loss* (vol. 2: Separation). New York: Basic Books.

Bozormenyi-Nagy, I., & Frame, J.L. (Eds.). (1966). *Intensive family therapy: Theoretical and practical aspects*. New York: Harper & Row.

Brockman, L., Whitely, J., & Zubec, J. (1973). *Child development: Selected readings*. Toronto: McClelland & Stewart.

Bronfenbrenner, U. (1968). Early deprivation in mammals: A cross-species analysis. In G. Newton & S. Levine (Eds.), *Early experience and behaviour*. Springfield, IL: C.C. Thomas.

Bronfenbrenner, U. (1970). *Two worlds of childhood*. New York: Russell Sage Foundation.

Brossard, M., & Decarie, T.G. (1971). The effects of three kinds of perceptual-social stimulation on the development of institutionalized infants: Preliminary report of a longitudinal study. *Early Childhood Development Care, 1*, 211–30.

Brown, W.K., & Rhodes, W.A. (1991). Factors that promote invulnerability and resiliency in at-risk children. In W.A. Rhodes & W.K. Brown (Eds.), *Why some children succeed despite the odds*. New York: Praeger.

Burlingham, D., & Freud, A. (1942). *Young children in wartime*. London: Allen & Unwin.

Caldwell, B.M. (1962). Mother – infant interaction in monomatric and polmatric families. *American Journal of Orthopsychiatry, 32*, 340–41.

Caldwell, B.M. (1964). The effects of infant care. In M.L. Hoffman & L.W. Hoffman (Eds.), *Review of child development research* (vol. 1). New York: Russell Sage Foundation.

Caldwell, B.M. (1968). The fourth dimension in early education. In R.D. Hess & R.M. Bear (Eds.), *Early education, current theory, research and action*. Chicago: Aldine.

Caldwell, B.M., Wright, C.M., Honig, A.C., & Tannenbaum, J. (1970). Infant day care and attachment. *American Journal Orthopsychiatry, 40*, 397–412.

Casler, L. (1961). Maternal deprivation: A critical review of the literature. *Monographs of the Society for Research on Child Development, 26* (2).

Casler, L. (1968). Perceptual deprivation in institutional settings. In G. Newton & S. Levine (Eds.), *Early experience and behaviour*. Springfield, IL: C.C. Thomas.

Clarke, A.D.B., & Clarke, A.M. (1960). Some recent advances in the study of early deprivation. *Journal of Child Psychology and Psychiatry, 1,* 26.

Clarke-Stewart, K. A. (1973). Interactions between mothers and their children: Characteristics and consequences. In *Monographs of the Society for Research on Child Development, 38,* 6–7.

Cohen, J.S., & Westhues, A. (1990). *Well-functioning families for adoptive and foster children.* Toronto: University of Toronto Press.

David, M., & Appell, G. (1961). A study of nursing care and nurse – infant interaction. A report on the first half on an investigation. In B.M. Foss (Ed.), *Determinants of infant behaviour* (vol. 1). London: Methuen.

Davis, C. (1966). *Room to grow: A study of parent–child relationships.* Toronto: University of Toronto Press.

De Chateau, Peter. (1991). A 30-year prospective follow-up study of 125 infants in child guidance clinics in Stockholm. *Infant Mental Health Journal, 12* (2), 116–125.

Dennis, W. (1973). *Children of the creche.* New York: Appleton-Century-Crofts.

Dennis, W., & Najarian, P. (1957). Infant development under environmental handicap. *Psychological Monographs, 71,* 1–13.

Deutsch, M., Katz, I., & Jensen, A. (Eds.). (1968). *Social class, race and psychological development.* New York: Holt, Rinehart & Winston.

Doll, E.A. (1953). *The measurement of social competence.* Minneapolis, MN: Educational Test Bureau.

Erikson, Eric. (1950). *Childhood and society.* New York: Norton.

Escalona, Sybile. (1968). *The roots of individuality.* New York: Aldine.

Flint, B.M. (1959). *The security of infants.* Toronto: University of Toronto Press.

Flint, B.M. (1966). *The child and the institution: A study of deprivation and recovery.* Toronto: University of Toronto Press.

Flint, B.M. (1970, Fall). Need kindergarten be too late? *Educational Theory, 20* (4), 399–406.

Flint, B.M. (1978). *New hope for deprived children.* Toronto: University of Toronto Press.

Flint, B.M. (1983). *Manual and scale: The Flint Infant Security Scale.* Toronto: Institute of Child Study, University of Toronto.

Freeman, F. (1962). *Theory and practice of psychological testing.* New York: Holt, Rinehart & Winston.

Frost, J. & Hawkes, G.R. (Eds.). (1970). *The disadvantaged child: Issues and innovations* (2nd ed.). Boston: Houghton Mifflin.

Furchner, C.S., & Harlow, H.F. (1969). Preference for various surrogate surfaces among infant rhesus monkeys. *Psychononomic Science, 17,* 279–80.

Gardner, D.B., Hawkes, G.R., & Burchinal, L.G. (1961). Non-continuous mothering in infancy and development in later childhood. *Child Development, 32,* 225–34.

Gardner, L.I. (1972). *Deprivation dwarfism in nature and nurture of behaviour: Readings from* Scientific American. San Francisco: W.H. Freeman.

Garmezy, N., & Rutter, M. (1989). *Stress, coping and development in children.* New York: McGraw-Hill.

Garmezy, N., Masten, A., Nordstrom, L., & Terroresse, M. (1979). The nature of competence in normal and deviant children. In M.W. Kent and J.E. Rolf (Eds.), *The primary prevention of psychopathology* (vol. 3). Hanover, NH: New England Press.

Garmezy, N., & Neuchterlein, K. (1972). Invulnerable children: The facts and fiction of competence and disadvantage. *American Journal of Orthopsychiatry, 42,* 328–29.

Gesell, A., & Amatruda, T. (1941). *Developmental diagnosis.* New York: P.B. Heeber.

Gewirts, J.L. (1968). The role of stimulation in models for child development. In L.L. Dittman (Ed.)., *Early child care: The new perspectives.* New York: Atherton Press.

Glasser, W. (1965). *Reality therapy.* New York: Harper & Row.

Goldfarb, W. (1943). Effects of early institutional care on adolescent personality. *Journal of Experiential Education, 12,* 106.

Goldfarb, W. (1945). Psychological privation in infancy and subsequent adjustment. *American Journal of Orthopsychiatry, 15,* 247–55.

Goldfarb, W. (1945). Effects of psychological deprivation in infancy and subsequent stimulation. *American Journal of Orthopsychiatry, 102,* 18–33.

Goldfarb, W. (1947). Variations in adolescent adjustment of institutionally reared children. *American Journal of Orthopsychiatry, 17,* 449–57.

Gordon, T. (1971). *Parent effectiveness training.* New York: P.H. Wyden.

Greenspan, S., Weider, S., Leiberman, A., Nover, R., Lourie, R., & Robinson, M. (1985). Infants in multi-risk families: Case studies of preventive intervention. *Clinical Infant Reports No. 3,* Mono. 47/48. New York: International Universities Press.

Greenspan, S., Weider, S., Poisson, S., & Lourie, R. (1988 April). Enduring gains: A five-year follow-up report on the clinical infant development program. In *Zero to three: Bulletin of the National Center for Clinical Infant Programs* (vol. VIII).

Gronlund, N.E. (1968). *Readings in measurement and evaluation.* New York: Macmillan.

Hajal, F., & Rosenburg, E. (1991). The family life cycles in adoptive families. *American Journal of Orthopsychiatry, 61* (1).

Harlow, H.F. (1958). The nature of love. *American Psychology, 13,* 673–85.

Harlow, H.F. (1961). The development of affectional patterns in infant monkeys. In B.M. Foss (Ed.), *Determinants of infant behaviour* (vol. 1). London: Methuen.

Harlow, H.F. (1963). The maternal affectional system. In B.M. Foss (Ed.), *Determinants of infant behaviour* (vol. 2). London: Methuen.

Harlow, H.F., & Harlow, M.K. (1969). Effects of various mother–infant relationships on rhesus monkey behaviour. In B.M. Foss (Ed.), *Determinants of infant behaviour* (vol. 4). London: Methuen.

Harlow, H.F., Schlitz, K.A., & Harlow, M.K. (1969). Effects of social isolation on the learning performance of rhesus monkeys. In *Proceedings of the Second Intternational Congress Primatology,* (vol. 1). Atlanta, GA: S. Karger.

Harlow, H.F., & Suomi, S.J. (1971). Social recovery by isolation reared monkeys. *Proceedings of the National Academy of Science, 68,* 1534–38.

Harlow, H.F., & Zimmermann, R.R. (1959). Affectional responses in the infant monkey. *Science, 130,* 421–32.

Harowitz, F. (Ed.). (1975). *Review of child development research* (vol. 4). Chicago: University of Chicago Press.

Hartrup, W. (Ed.). (1982). *Review of child development research* (vol. 6). Chicago: University of Chicago Press.

Harway, M. (1984). Confidentiality and ethics in longitudinal research. In S.A. Mednick & B. Mednick (Eds.), *A handbook of longitudinal research,* (vol 1). New York: Praeger.

Haywood, C. (1967). Experimental factors in intellectual development: The concept of dynamic intelligence. In T. Zubin & G.A. Jervis (Eds.), *Psychopathology in mental development.* New York: Grune & Stratton.

Hebb, D.O. (1949). *The organization of behaviour.* New York: Wiley.

Hinde, R.A. (1976). Interactions, relationships, and social structure. *Man, 11,* 1–7.

Hollingshead, A.W. (1949). *The index of social position.* New Haven: Yale University Press.

Howells, J.G. (Ed.). (1971). *Modern perspectives in international child psychiatry.* New York: Brunner/Mazel.

Hunt, J. McV. (1972). (Abstract). Early childhood education and social class. *The Canadian Psychologist, 13* (4). Canadian Psychological Association, University of Calgary.

Jensen, A.R. (1969). How much can we boost IQ and scholastic achievement? *Harvard Ed_u_cucational Review, 39,* 1–123.

Jones, M.C., Bayley, N., MacFarlane, J.W., & Honzik, M.P. (Eds.). (1971). *The course of human development.* Waltham, MA: Xerox College Publishing.

Kagan, J. (1971). *Change and continuity in infancy.* New York: Wiley & Sons.

Kagan, J., & Moss, H. (1962). *A study in psychological development: A prediction of behavior from birth to maturity.* New York: Wiley.

Kilgour, M. (1963). *The Jones family.* Available from Catholic Children's Aid Society of Metro Toronto.

Klackenberg, G. (1956). Studies on maternal deprivation in infants' homes. *Acta Paediatrica Scandinavica, 45,* 1–12.

Lally, J.R., Mangione, P., Honig, A., & Wittner, D. (1988, April). More pride, less delinquency: Findings from the ten-year follow-up study of the Syracuse University Family Development Research Program. In *Zero to three: Bulletin of the National Center for Clinical Infant Programs* (vol. VIII).

Lamb, M. (Ed.). (1981). *The role of the father in child development.* New York: Wiley.

Langmeier, J., & Matycek, Z. (1970). Mental development of children in families and in infants' homes. *Social Science and Medicine, 4,* 569–77.

Leifer, A.D., Leiderman, P.H., Barnet, C.R., & Williams, J.A. (1972). Effects of mother–infant separation on maternal attachment behavior. *Child Development, 43* (4).

Lewis, M. (1979). *The social network: Toward a theory of social development.* Fiftieth Anniversary Invited Address. Eastern Psychological Association Meeting.

Lewis, M., & Rosenblum, L. (1974). *The effect of the infant on its caregiver.* New York: John Wiley & Sons.

Lowney, L.G. (1940). Personality distortion and early institutional care. *American Journal of Orthopsychiatry, 10,* 576.

Luthar, S., & Zigler, E. (1991). Vulnerability and competence: A review of research on resilience in childhood. *American Journal of Orthopsychiatry, 61* (1).

Maas, H.S. (1963). The young adult adjustment of twenty wartime residential nursery children. *Child Welfare, 42,* 42–57.

Maccoby, E., & Masters, J.C. (1970). Attachment and dependency. In P.H. Mussen (Ed.), *Carmichael's manual of child psychology* (3rd ed.). New York: Wiley.

Richards, M.P. (Ed.). (1974). *The integration of the child into the social world.* Cambridge: Cambridge University Press.

Mead, M. (1962). A cultural anthropologist's approach to maternal deprivation. In *Deprivation of maternal care: A reassessment of its effects.* Geneva: World Health Organization.

Mednick, S.A., & Baert, A.E. (1981). *Prospective longitudinal research: An empirical basis for primary prevention of psychosocial disorders.* Oxford Medical Publications, Oxford University Press. Copenhagen: World Health Organization Regional Offices for Europe.

Mednick, S., Harway, M., & Finello, K. (Eds.). (1984). *A handbook of longitudinal research* (vols. i–ii). New York: Praeger.

Mednick, S.A., & Mednick, B. (1984). A brief history of North American longitudinal research. In S.A. Mednick, M. Harway, & K. Finello (Eds.), *A handbook of longitudinal research* (vol. i). New York: Praeger.

Meeker, M.N. (1969). *The structure of the intellect.* Columbus, OH: Merrill.

Meisels, S.J., & Shonkoff, J.P. (Eds.). (1990). *A handbook of early childhood intervention.* Cambridge: Cambridge University Press.

Morgan, P. (1975). *Child care, sense and fable.* London: Temple Smith.

Moriarty, A.E. (1966). *Constancy and I.Q. change.* Springfield, IL: C.C. Thomas.

Murphy, L.B., & Moriarty, A.E. (1976). *Vulnerability, coping and growth.* New Haven: Yale University Press.

Newton, G., & Levine, S. (Eds.). (1968). *Early experience and behaviour: The psychobiology of development.* Springfield, IL: C.C. Thomas.

Nicol, A.R. (Ed.). (1985). *Longitudinal studies in child psychology and psychiatry: Practical lessons from research experience.* Chichester, New York & Toronto: John Wiley & Sons.

Patton, T.G., & Gardner, L.I. (1963). *Growth failure in maternal deprivation.* Springfield, IL: C.C. Thomas.

Piaget, J. (1952). *The origins of intelligence in children.* New York: International Universities Press.

Piaget, J., & Inhelder, B. (1969). *The psychology of the child.* New York: Basic Books.

Prahl-Anderson, B.E., Kowalski, C., & Heyendael, P. (Eds.). (1979). *A mixed longitudinal interdisciplinary study of growth and development.* London: Academic Press.

Prechtl, H.F.R. (1963). The mother–child interaction in babies with minimal brain damage. In B.M. Foss (Ed.), *Determinants of infant behaviour* (vol. 2). London: Methuen.

Pringle, M.L. (1966). *Social learning and its measurement.* London: Longmans.

Pringle, M.L., & Bossio, V. (1958). Intellectual, emotional, and social development of deprived children. *Vita Human, 1,* 66–92.

Pringle, M.L., & Bossio, V. (1960). Early prolonged separations and emotional adjustment. *Journal of Child Psychology and Psychiatry, 1,* 37–48.

Provence, S., & Lipton, R.C. (1962). *Infants in institutions.* New York: International Universities Press.

Provence, S., & Ritvo, S. (1961). Deprivation in institutionalized infants. *Psychoanalytical Studies of Childhood, 26,* 189. New York: International Universities Press.

Rapaport, D. (1961). *Diagnostic psychological testing* (vol. 1). Chicago: Year Book Publications.

Rheingold, H.L. (1956). The modification of social responsiveness in institutional babies. *Monographs of the Society for Research on Child Development, 21* (63).

Rheingold, H.L. (1961). The effect of environmental stimulation upon social and exploratory behaviour in the human infant. In B.M. Foss (Ed.), *Determinants of infant behaviour* (vol. 1). London: Methuen.

Rheingold, H.L., & Bayley, N. (1959). The later effects of an experimental modification of mothering. *Child Development, 30,* 363–72.

Rheingold, H.L., Gewirtz, J., & Ross, H. (1959). Social conditioning of vocalizations in the infant. *Journal of Comparative Physiology and Psychology, 52,* 68–73.

Rhodes, W.E., & Brown, W. (Eds.). (1991). *Why some children succeed despite the odds.* New York: Praeger.

Ribble, M. (1944). *Infantile experience in relation to personality development: Personality and the behaviour disorders.* New York: Columbia University Press.

Riese, H. (1962). *Healing the hurt child.* Chicago: University of Chicago Press.

Robertson, J. (1952). *A two-year-old goes to hospital* [16 mm sound film with guidebook]. Tavistock Child Development Research Unit.

Robertson, J., & Bowlby, J. (1952). Responses of young children to separation from their mothers. *Courier Centre International Enfants,* 131–142. Paris: UNESCO.

Robertson, J., & Robertson, J. (1967a). *Young children in brief separation: I. Kate, aged two years, five months in fostercare for twenty-seven days.* Tavistock Child Development Research Unit.

Robertson, J., & Robertson, J. (1967b). *Young children in brief separation: II. Jane, aged seventeen months in fostercare for ten days.* Tavistock Child Development Research Unit.

Robins, L.N. (1966). *Deviant children grown up.* Baltimore: Williams & Wilkins.

Robins, L.N. (1984). Longitudinal methods in the study of development. In S.A. Mednick, M. Harway, & K. Finello (Eds.), *A handbook of longitudinal research* (vol. 1). New York: Praeger.

Rosenthal, R., & Jacobson, L.F. (1968). *Pygmalion in the classroom: teacher expectation and pupils' intellectual development.* New York: Holt, Rinehart & Winston.

Roudinesco, J. (1952). Severe maternal deprivation and personality development in early childhood. *Understanding the Child, 21* (4).

Rutter, M. (1972). *Maternal deprivation reassessed.* Harmondsworth: Penguin Books.

Rutter, M. (1987, July). Psychological resilience and protective mechanisms. *American Journal of Orthopsychiatry, 57* (3).

Rutter, M. (1989). Pathways from childhood to adult life. *Journal of Psychology and Psychiatry, 30* (1), 23–51.

Rutter, M. (1990). Psychosocial resilience and protective mechanisms. In J. Rolf, A.S. Masten, D. Chichetti, K. Neuchterlein, & S. Weintraub (Eds.), *Risk and protective factors in the development of psychopathology.* Cambridge and New York: Cambridge University Press.

Rutter, M., & Quinton, D. (1981). Longitudinal studies of institutional children and children of mentally ill parents. In S.A. Mednick & A.E. Baert (Eds.), *Prospective longitudinal research: An empirical basis for the primary prevention of psychosocial disorders.* Oxford: Oxford University Press.

Rutter, M., & Nicola, M. (1976). *Cycles of disadvantage.* London: Heinemann.

Ryan, T.J. (1972). *Poverty and the child.* Toronto: McGraw-Hill Ryerson.

Schaffer, H.R. (Ed.). (1969). *The origins of human relations.* New York: Academic Press.

Schaffer, H.R. (1971a). *The growth of sociability.* Harmondsworth: Penguin Books.

Schaffer, H.R. (1971b). *The origin of human social relations.* Proceedings of Conference, London, 1969. London & New York: Academic Press.

Schaffer, H.R. (Ed.). (1977). *Studies in mother–infant interaction.* London: Academic Press.

Scott, J.P. (1968). *Early experience and the organization of behavior.* Belmont, MA: Brooks/Cole Publishing.

Scrimshaw, N.D., & Gordon, J.E. (1968). *Malnutrition, learning and behavior.* Cambridge, MA: MIT Press.

Siegel, Sidney (1956). *Non-parametric statistics for the behavioral sciences.* New York: McGraw-Hill.

Skeels, H.M. (1966). Adult status of children with contrasting early life experiences. *Monographs of the Society for Research on Child Development, 31.*

Skodak, M., & Skeels, H.M. (1949). A final follow-up study of one hundred adopted children. *Journal of Genetics and Psychology, 75,* 85–125.

Spitz, R.A. (1945). Hospitalism: An enquiry into the genesis of psychiatric conditions in early childhood. *Psychoanalytic Study of the Child, 1,* 53–74.

Steinhauer, Paul. (1991). *The least detrimental alternative.* Toronto: University of Toronto Press.

Stone, L.J., Murphy, L.B., & Smith, H.T. (Eds.). (1973). *The competent infant.* New York: Basic Books.

Taylor, A. (1968a). Institutionalized infants' concept formation ability. *American Journal of Orthopsychiatry, 38,* 110.

Taylor, A. (1968b). Deprived infants: Potential for affective adjustment. *American Journal of Orthopsychiatry, 38* (5), 835–45.

Taylor, A. (1970). Follow-up of institutionalized infants' concept formation ability at age 12. *American Journal of Orthopsychiatry, 40* (3), 141–47.

Thomas, A., & Chess, S. (1977). *Temperament and development.* New York: Brunner/Mazel.

Thomas, A., Chess, S., & Birch, H.G. (1968). *Temperament and behavior disorders in children.* New York: New York University Press.

Tizard, B., & Hodges, J. (1978). The effect of early institutional rearing on the development of eight-year-old children. *Journal Child Psychology and Psychiatry, 19,* 99–118.

Tizard, J. (1969). The role of social institutions in the causation, prevention, and alleviation of mental retardation. In C. Hayward (Ed.), *Socio-cultural aspects of mental retardation.* New York: Academic Press.

Tizard, J., & Tizard, B. (1971). The social development of two-year-old children in residential nurseries. In H.R. Schaffer (Ed.), *The origins of human social relations.* New York: Academic Press.

Tizard, J., & Tizard, B. (1972). The institution as an environment for development. In M.P. Richards (Ed.), *The integration of a child into a social world.* New York: Academic Press.

Trasler, G. (1960). *In place of parents: A study of foster care.* London: Routledge & Kegan Paul.

Turner, F.J. (Ed.). *Differential diagnosis and treatment in social work, Part I. Stages of human development. Part II. Psychosocial pathology.* New York: The Free Press.

Warner, L., Havinghurst, R., & Loeb, M. (1944). *Who shall be educated?* New York: Harper Bros.

Werner, E.E. (1985). Stress and protective factors in children's lives. In A.R. Nichol (Ed.), *Longitudinal studies in child psychology and psychiatry.* Chichester: John Wiley & Sons.

Werner, E.E. (1988, April). Individual differences, universal needs: A 30-year study of resilient high-risk infants. In *Zero to three: bulletin of the National Center for Clinical Infant Programs* (vol. VIII).

Werner, E.E. (1990). Protective factors and individual resilience. In S.J. Meisels & J.P. Shonkoff (Eds.), *A handbook of early childhood intervention.* Cambridge: Cambridge University Press.

Werner, E.E., & Smith, R.S. (1982). *Vulnerable but invincible.* Toronto: McGraw-Hill.

White, B.L. (1971). *Human infants: Experience and psychological development.* Englewood Cliffs, NJ: Prentice-Hall.

Woodland, Martin. (1988). When psychology informs public policy. *The American Psychologist, 4* (6), 443–54.

Wrede, C., Byring, R., Enberg, S., Huttunen, M., Mednick, S.A., & Nilsson, C.G. (1981). A longitudinal study of a risk group in Finland. In S.A. Mednick and A.E. Baert (Eds.), *Prospective longitudinal research: An empirical basis for the primary prevention of psychological disorders.* Oxford: Oxford University Press.

Yarrow, L.J. (1961). Maternal deprivation: Toward an empirical and conceptual re-evaluation. *Psychological Bulletin, 58,* 459–90.

Yarrow, L.J. (1963). Research in dimensions of early maternal care. *Merrill–Palmer Quarterly, 9,* 101–14.

Yarrow, L.J. (1964). Separation from parents during early childhood. In M.L. Hoffman & L.W. Hoffman (Eds.), *Review of child development research* (vol. 1). New York: Russell Sage Foundation.

Index